Improve your ENGLISH

ENGLISH

in the WORKPLACE

Improve your ENGLISH

ENGLISH in the WORKPLACE

Stephen E. Brown and Ceil Lucas

New York   Chicago   San Francisco   Lisbon   London   Madrid   Mexico City
Milan   New Delhi   San Juan   Seoul   Singapore   Sydney   Toronto

3 4 5 6 7 8 9 10 11 12 13 14 15 16 17 18 19   DOC/DOC   1 5 4 3 2 1

ISBN   978-0-07-149718-3 (book and DVD)
MHID   0-07-149718-8 (book and DVD)

ISBN   978-0-07-149719-0 (book alone)
MHID   0-07-149719-6 (book alone)

Library of Congress Control Number: 2007941298

McGraw-Hill books are available at special quantity discounts to use as premiums and sales promotions or for use in corporate training programs. To contact a representative, please visit the Contact Us pages at www.mhprofessional.com.

Note: Views expressed in the DVD are those of the interviewees and do not necessarily reflect the views of the authors/editors or the publisher.

Also in this series:

Improve Your English: English in Everyday Life
Improve Your American English Accent

This book is printed on acid-free paper.

CONTENTS

ACKNOWLEDGMENTS

We are very grateful to Patrick Harris for his excellent work filming and editing the DVDs. We thank all of the people who were willing to be interviewed and also Holly McGuire, Christopher Brown, and Julia Anderson Bauer of McGraw-Hill Professional; Jim Dellon, Ivey Wallace, and Jayne McKenzie of Gallaudet University; Kevin Keegan of Hubert Blake High School in Silver Spring, Maryland; Mike Solano and Merchant's Tire in Laurel, Maryland; and Jim Smith, Kim MacKenzie Smith, and The Skydivin' Place in Kingsdale, Pennsylvania.

INTRODUCTION

English in the Workplace consists of ninety-one interview segments with everyday people, not actors, speaking English in the United States. The interviews are organized into ten chapters. Each chapter focuses on a different aspect of work, from looking for work and interviewing for jobs to communicating and using technology at work. The goal in using an interview format was to elicit natural speech and to allow the speakers to express themselves as freely and naturally as possible. In these interviews, you will hear the vocabulary and sentence structures that real speakers use to talk about their working lives.

Because we wanted to provide learners of English with natural models of spoken English in the United States, those being interviewed did not memorize or rehearse their remarks. You will meet people of all ages and nationalities, from all walks of life: a policeman, a nurse, accountants, a paramedic, a student, teachers, a librarian, a mechanic, an IT professional, a travel agent, a sign language interpreter, musicians, and others.

Each chapter includes the complete transcript of each interview segment as well as definitions of vocabulary words, idioms, and constructions whose meanings or cultural references may not be immediately obvious to a nonnative English speaker. You will find questions and exercises at the end of each chapter that are relevant to both the text of the interview and your own personal experiences. We recommend that you consult a comprehensive American English dictionary in conjunction with the use of the DVD and workbook.

ABOUT THE TRANSCRIPTS

What you will hear on the DVD and see in the transcripts are examples of actual speech. Our goal is to provide examples of English as it is spoken by a wide range of people in the United States today. You will hear speakers from many states—Maryland, New Jersey, Massachusetts, Arkansas, Illinois, Maine, Minnesota, and Michigan—as well as speakers from Canada, India, Guyana, England, New Zealand, Cameroon, Egypt, and Spain. Also, you will hear one speaker whose speech has many features of what is known as African-American Vernacular English (AAVE). So you will hear English spoken with many different accents. You will also see a deaf user of American Sign Language (ASL) with her interpreter.

You will notice that while all of the speakers are fluent, they sometimes use what some consider nonstandard or even ungrammatical forms of English. And you will see that not only do the nonnative speakers use these forms, but native speakers of American English frequently use them as well. Some of these speakers are very fluent users of varieties of English used in other countries, such as India, varieties that have been referred to as "World Englishes" and that differ from American or British English in very systematic and nonrandom ways.

You will notice that when people speak, it is not at all like a newscast being read by an anchorperson on the evening news or like the written language that you might see in textbooks. You will see that people don't always speak in complete sentences—they hesitate; they interrupt themselves; they correct themselves; they start one sentence, give it up, and go on with another one. While the speakers clearly knew that they were being filmed, what you see and hear is, for the most part, very natural speech. Our goal was to reflect this naturalness in the transcripts. Interjections and discourse markers such as *um*, *uh*, or *er* appear throughout the interviews and are transcribed exactly as they are spoken. Sometimes people talk at the same time, which is indicated in the transcripts by brackets around the simultaneous speech.

The transcripts also reflect the use of many customary and idiomatic constructions found in American English: *take it up a notch, so-and-so, such and such, like, y'know, c'mon, gonna, wanna, I gotchu*, and many others. Notes explaining such constructions appear at the end of each chapter.

It is our hope that you will find these materials innovative and useful for learning English as it is used in America today.

How to Use These Materials in the Classroom

The DVD and workbook of *English in the Workplace* have been designed for use in any classroom, laboratory, or home setting. These materials, which are suitable for high school classes, university courses, and adult education programs, can be used as the second semester of an elementary course.

The way that language is used by speakers in these materials can serve as the basis for both in-class discussions and homework assignments.

The DVD and the workbook provide ninety-one segments, which should be used as follows:

1. Select the segment to be used and simply *listen* to it, *before* reading the transcript of the segment. The

student can do this on his or her own or as part of a classroom activity.

2. After listening to the segment, *read* and *discuss* the transcript carefully, making sure that all of the vocabulary words and structures are understood.
3. Then, *listen* to the segment again, this time using the transcript. Students may want to listen to the segment several times at this point.
4. In the classroom, answer and discuss the questions about both the segment and the students' experiences. And, of course, these questions and exercises can be assigned for homework.

Outlining a Course by DVD Segments

The instructor can decide how many segments to cover per week. DVD segments allow you to use the DVD and the workbook for an entire academic year. And the flexibility of the materials allows you to pick and choose the order in which to present the material. Each segment on the DVD is numbered on the menu and in the text so that you can pick exactly which one you want to focus on.

Sample Lesson Plan: One Week

First Day: Listen to the selected segments perhaps two or three times in class (do not read the transcript at this point).

Second Day: Read the transcript out loud, making sure that the students understand all of the grammatical constructions, vocabulary words, and cultural references.

Third Day: Listen to the segments again, first without the transcript and then with the transcript.

Fourth Day: Discuss the transcript and the DVD segment and answer the questions pertaining to the segment. Assign as homework the questions and exercises that pertain to the students.

Fifth Day: Go over the questions and exercises pertaining to the students. Ask them to read their answers aloud, and have the class ask them additional questions.

The DVD segments and their transcripts can very easily be supplemented with materials that relate to the topic of the segment. For example, the segments on Looking for Work can be supplemented with want ads from the local newspaper or from the Web, the segments on Dressing for Work can be supplemented with photos from a variety of sources of people in their work clothes, and so forth. The important thing is to be creative and to get the students involved.

Additional Activities

1. Ask the students to summarize in writing and also aloud what is said in a given segment.
2. Ask the students to write the question that leads to the speaker's response. Also, ask them to write additional questions to be asked.
3. Have the students interview one another on the topic of the segment in front of the class:
   - Help the students write their interview questions.
   - If possible, record these interviews on audiotape or miniDV. Listen to or view the interviews and discuss them as a group.
   - Have the students transcribe these interviews, complete with hesitations, self-corrections, and so forth. Make copies of the transcript for the other students. The teacher may review the transcript but should make corrections only to errors in transcription—in other words, if the speaker

uses a nonstandard form and the student transcribes it accurately, you should not note it as an error. This is a good opportunity to point out the differences between spoken language and written language.

- Have the students write questions about their transcripts, similar to the ones in the text.
- Have the students record an interview with a native or fluent speaker, based on one of the DVD topics, and follow the same procedures just listed. Help the students prepare their questions, review the transcripts, and share them with the class. Also, ask the students to write questions to accompany their transcripts.

CHAPTER 1

WHAT KIND OF WORK DO YOU DO?

Part I

In this chapter, all of the interviewees briefly state what kind of jobs they have.

1. THE LIBRARIAN

I work at the U.S. Library of Congress in Washington, D.C., and I work in a department at the library that's called the Congressional Research Service. We are sort of like a little think tank that works for the Congress of the United States, and we provide information and assistance to members of Congress and the committees

of Congress as they're developing legislation and working on policy issues that get enacted into law. My specialty area is the environment, particularly, uh, water
pollution issues. So anything that has to do with water
pollution of United States—rivers, lakes, streams, et
cetera—I might have, I might be of some assistance to
members of Congress when they're trying to write new
laws.

2. THE NURSE

Uh, I'm actually a, uh, nurse—a **registered nurse**—and
also a businessman.

3. THE ARTIST

Today, um, I have some art projects and I have some
speaking projects where I write on different topics.
Recently I gave the-the lecture, 'cause of my interest in
military history, on Iwo Jima and comparisons between
Gallipoli, which is the ANZAC Day, an important day for
Australians and New Zealanders, and, uh, a comparison
with Iwo Jima, very similar campaigns at many different levels. So I do—I'm self-employed—I do a mixture of
everything that I can to survive.

4. THE CHEMIST

I work at the **Environmental Protection Agency** and I
run a number of programs.

5. THE MECHANIC

Uh, I work at Merchant's Tire—er, um, put tires on cars, do oil changes, do alignments for cars, make sure they drive straight, drive straight, drive well.

6. THE OFFICE MANAGER

Uh, right now, I'm the manager of the Purchasing Department.

7. THE SIGN LANGUAGE TEACHER

[Note: The voice you hear is that of the interpreter, on the right, who is interpreting for the deaf woman, on the left, who is signing American Sign Language.]

Right now, I'm working **part-time** teaching **ASL**, American Sign Language, here at Gallaudet University, in the evenings. I'm teaching ASL 3.

8. THE RETIRED POLICEMAN

RETIRED POLICEMAN: What do I do now?

INTERVIEWER: Yes.

RETIRED POLICEMAN: I'm retired.

INTERVIEWER: Oh. Retired from what?

RETIRED POLICEMAN: Well, actually it was two jobs—but I did the two jobs at the same time at one point. My main job was a Maryland state police officer and, after working the roads for fifteen years, I became a helicopter pilot for the state police. So I flew a helicopter my last nine years with the state police and, when I retired, then I went to work for a hospital in Washington, D.C., and flew a medical helicopter for them for eleven years—a little over eleven years.

INTERVIEWER: Other than those two?

RETIRED POLICEMAN: You mean in my lifetime?

INTERVIEWER: Yeah.

RETIRED POLICEMAN: Oh, **jeez**.

INTERVIEWER: What other jobs?

RETIRED POLICEMAN: I was a farmhand, a carpenter's helper, a bricklayer's helper, I worked in a, ice cream, you know the, like a Tastee Freez or whatever. I've worked cleaning furnaces—when I was in the state police—I did that on the side, just for extra money. Uh, what else? Well, teaching flying. I've taught flying for thirty years. Uh, jeez, I don't know.

9. THE UNIVERSITY PROFESSOR (LINGUISTICS)

UNIVERSITY PROFESSOR: I'm a professor in the Linguistics Department at Gallaudet University.

INTERVIEWER: And what kind of university is that?

UNIVERSITY PROFESSOR: It's a small **liberal arts college**. Um, it serves deaf and hard of hearing students.

10. THE ENTREPRENEUR AND THE SURGICAL TECHNOLOGIST

ENTREPRENEUR: Uh, as little as possible. I guess if you had to put one-word title on it, entrepreneur. Uh, some small business, mini-storage development, running the skydiving school, tattoo and body piercing studio, some investment properties, residential, commercial rentals.

SURGICAL TECHNOLOGIST: I work in an operating room. I'm a surgical technologist.

11. THE TRAVEL AGENT

Um, I'm a travel agent—I take care of international ticketing and cruises and tours—basically, vacation management.

12. THE CPA AND THE **IT** PROFESSIONAL

CPA: During the week, I'm an accountant and, on the weekends, I'm a zookeeper.

INTERVIEWER: And how 'bout you?

IT PROFESSIONAL: I'm an IT professional at a company called, um, it was originally called Argus Group when I just started working there and they've had a—what's called a spin-off—I'm not too familiar what exactly it is but, uh, um, so the company is now called Broadridge and that was a subsidiary of a company called ADP . . .

INTERVIEWER: Uh-huh.

IT PROFESSIONAL: . . . which is a huge company known all throughout the world, uh, with something over 42,000 employees. And I work in the IT department there, so I do some programming.

13. THE **EMT**

I'm in **EMS** work, in the EMS field, I teach, um, and train, um, people who work on the ambulance—EMTs—and I also work in an emergency room.

14. THE UNIVERSITY PROFESSOR (ARCHAEOLOGY AND ANTIQUITIES)

I'm a classics professor. I, uh, uh, my background is in, um, ancient language, Latin language and Latin literature, and ancient history, Roman in particular, uh, but also ancient Greek. I am also a Roman archaeologist. And so I teach, uh, I teach in all of these areas—uh, Latin language, uh, ancient history, and Roman archaeology.

15. THE SIGN LANGUAGE INTERPRETER

Well, I'm currently employed as a sign language interpreter. I'm working in private practice and I also consult with various companies around the United States, particularly in the area, here in the Washington, D.C., area. As well, I teach interpreting, I teach sign language interpreting to students at a local **community college**.

16. THE ACADEMIC ADVISOR/HOTEL MANAGER

ACADEMIC ADVISOR: I'm academic advisor at the embassy.

INTERVIEWER: Which embassy?

ACADEMIC ADVISOR: United Arab Emirates.

INTERVIEWER: Oh. How long have you been doing that?

ACADEMIC ADVISOR: Almost ten years.

17. THE PROFESSIONAL MUSICIANS

HORN PLAYER: I work as a professional musician. I play French horn in orchestras, uh, in the Maryland-Baltimore-Washington area.

INTERVIEWER: And Lysiane?

VIOLINIST: Uh, well, I do about the same work that Paul do, uh, except that I play violin, but I'm also a **freelance** musician around Washington-Baltimore. I go to Delaware quite frequently as well.

DEFINITIONS

ASL (American Sign Language): A form of manual communication used by deaf and hard of hearing people in the United States. ASL is an autonomous linguistic system structurally independent from English. It is different from sign languages used in other countries, such as Italian Sign Language and Japanese Sign Language.

community college: A comparatively small institution of higher learning in the United States that usually provides two-year degrees and certifications in various academic, paraprofessional, and vocational fields.

EMS (Emergency Medical Service): A field of health care that focuses on providing emergency medical care to sick or injured individuals. The term *EMS* is usually used in reference to those who first respond to an accident or a crisis (first responders), such as EMTs or paramedics.

EMT (Emergency Medical Technician): An allied health professional who is responsible for responding to medical emergencies and providing initial first-aid care and transportation of the sick or injured persons to a medical facility.

Environmental Protection Agency (EPA): An agency of the U.S. federal government that is responsible for protecting human health and safeguarding the environment.

freelance: Employment in which people find their own work and go from job to job without a long-term work schedule.

IT (Information Technology): Equipment, devices, or infrastructure used for transmitting, storing, or processing electronic data.

jeez: A common discourse marker or expression of surprise or amazement. Short for *Jesus* or *Jesus Christ*.

liberal arts college: A kind of educational institution beyond high school in the United States, in which the undergraduates are required to take a wide range of courses in addition to specializing in one specific area of study before they are awarded a degree.

part-time: When referring to employment, usually defined as a job that is performed for fewer than forty hours per week.

registered nurse: A licensed medical professional who usually provides patient care under the direction of a physician.

QUESTIONS AND EXERCISES

1. List the jobs described in this chapter.

2. Which job described in this chapter requires the most education?

3. Which jobs require interaction with the public?

4. What kind of schedules are required by the jobs described in this chapter?

5. List the jobs of people you know.

6. Describe the jobs you have had.

7. Identify three words or phrases in this chapter that are new to you, and write a sentence with each one.

WHAT KIND OF WORK DO YOU DO?

PART II

In this chapter, some of the interviewees elaborate on the kind of work they do.

1. THE CHEMIST

One program I run for the **EPA** is the, what's called the lead paint program. Children in the United States are poisoned by lead from lead paint and we do a lot of work in conjunction with the Centers for Disease Control, uh, and other agencies such as **HUD** to minimize exposure to these children from lead paint; uh, we do a lot of **outreach**; we, uh, train and certify workers so that people will go in to get rid of the lead and know what they're doing; we look at other sources of lead that children will be exposed to. A recent big issue is lead in toy jewelry. Kids get this, a lot of hand to mouth, sometimes they swallow it; a child recently died, um, it-it was just horrible. There's no reason for children to be exposed to lead paint anymore but they are, and it affects them for a long time, for the rest of their lives. I also run a program on mercury, also the issue of mercury in products, a lot of international work associated with that, which is really interesting; um, I get to deal with a lot of different people from around the world, working with the United Nations Environment Program, they have a big action on mercury. So I'm particularly working on not only mercury in products but getting rid of some of the sources of mercury in the United States so that the demand gets reduced because mercury becomes more expensive.

Also phasing out products so you reduce the demand. So getting at it from-from both, uh, ends. I also run a program on **PCBs**, um, which, you know, are in the fish everywhere and particularly from the part of the country where I am from—uh, the **Great Lakes**—it's a big issue so we just try to reduce exposures from PCBs. Those are the three big programs that I run, and it's really quite interesting, it's a variety of issues. And I think the one, though, that I feel the strongest about is the lead poisoning, just-just because kids are just damaged for the rest of their life from lead—and it's something, um, they shouldn't have to be—there's no excuse in a developed country like ours, that we don't deal with that.

2. THE ACCOUNTANT

ACCOUNTANT: I'm a partner in a **CPA** firm here in-in Washington.

INTERVIEWER: How long have you been doing that?

ACCOUNTANT: I've been doing that for a little more than ten years.

3. THE NURSE

I, uh, currently, uh, and when I say "I," my wife and I, uh, we own, uh, this, uh, transportation company—uh, it's called Grace Transportation and Medical Services, GTMS—and we provide, uh, transportation, nonemergency transportation, uh, say from hospital to hospital or from home to hospital. You have somebody on **dialysis** that needs to go frequently to a dialysis center and we do that, but strictly, uh, stretcher, uh, transportation, so we're not doing wheelchair transportation and also, for example, if the hospital discharges a patient that needs to return to the nursing home, uh, they will give us a call and then we will do that. Our goal eventually is to **expantiate** on this and become what we call **ALS** also. Now we're **BLS**, which is **Basic Life Support**, so, uh, the most we can do with a patient is give them oxygen and make sure they're stable behind the ambulance truck. But once we go ALS, which is **Advanced Life Support**, then you have the liberty, of course, with the direction of a medical director, to administer drugs in cases of emergency; you can actually answer some **911** calls if you are in the jurisdiction that, uh, the calls came from.

4. THE LIBRARIAN

Working for an organization as large as the Congress—there are 535 members, there are several hundred committees, hundreds and hundreds of staff people—and they all have access to, uh, my services, the information that I have as well as information of the colleagues that I work with. We have people in my organization who deal with legal issues, who deal with social services kinds of issues—really—foreign affairs, uh, governmental policies and procedures, anything that the Congress might be interested in, they can call us, ask for information, ask for advice on how to craft a piece of legislation, um, or they may call up wanting to know why does this particular thing work the way that it does or-or not—variety of things like that, but they-they all have access to us.

5. THE RETIRED POLICEMAN

RETIRED POLICEMAN: Uh, police department or the flying part of it?

INTERVIEWER: Both of them.

RETIRED POLICEMAN: Uh, well, the police department part of it was interesting because you got to see a side of life that most people don't see. And sometimes I'll tell people things that happened on the police department and they don't believe you, they just don't think people are capable of doing some bad things. And then I've seen a lot of good things that people do, too.

But, uh, you just don't really understand what goes on in life when you're—people live in a little community, a **gated community** where they're away from the poverty and everything else—and they-they may be living comfortably and here's people in a city that don't have much and all kinds of crime and drugs and all that business and you think, "**There but for the grace of God go I.**" And I **wasn't**, you know, uh, I was raised on a farm and we didn't have much money but I think everybody in their lifetime comes to a point where they say, "Well, I can go this route or I can go the other route," and, uh, sometimes the route that leads to crimes might be a lot of money in it or, uh, **what have you**, but then you've got all the other stuff that goes with it where if you go the other route, you may not be **driving a Cadillac**, but, you know, but the police department part of it was pretty interesting. Whether I would do it again or not, I don't know.

6. THE PROFESSIONAL MUSICIANS

VIOLINIST: Ah, you know, every week is different and that's what we like best about our job is one week we're doing chamber orchestra, the next week it can be orchestra, big orchestra, ah, we do a lot of opera, ah—Paul does a lot of quintet—but you can talk about your quintet.

HORN PLAYER: I-I run a brass quintet, uh, which is made of two trumpets, a horn, trombone, and tuba. And we play a variety of different events—we play for people's weddings, uh, we do graduation ceremonies, uh, corporate events, um, uh, parties, all kinds of different stuff. Sometimes we'll play classical music for that, sometimes we'll play **pops music**; uh, we do educational programming also. And, uh, I actually run that group so I-I **book** the, uh, **the dates** that we perform, I work with the clients directly, I hire the musicians, um, and provide the sheet music for the people to play and, uh, try and keep things **running smoothly** as much as possible.

INTERVIEWER: So how long have you been professional musicians?

HORN PLAYER: Um, I'd, well, I-I did my first paid job right when I was graduating high school at eighteen and I am about to turn thirty-nine now, um, but I-I guess probably around 1990; '89 is when I really started to play, uh, more regular-regularly professionally.

VIOLINIST: Yeah, I guess, I guess I did my first professional jobs when I was either a junior or senior in college, which was '96, '97, so it's been **a good ten years**, uh, and it's always been in this area, which is great.

INTERVIEWER: And you also teach, don't you, and have an involvement with the schools?

HORN PLAYER: That's right, that's right, I have, um, a couple of private students that come here to my house, uh, and I give them, uh, private instruction on the French horn, and I also teach at Shepherd University in Shepherdstown, West Virginia—that's about an hour from here—um, uh I'm **adjunct faculty** there. I teach one day a week; uh, it's a **part-time** job, uh, and it just supplements the income that I make from performing on a regular basis.

7. THE HIGH SCHOOL STUDENT

HIGH SCHOOL STUDENT: Yeah, um, I used to think I knew completely but I don't. People always tell me I should become a lawyer 'cause I like to argue a lot but I would, I would really like to, um, become maybe an editor like my mom 'cause I'm on the newspaper at school and, um, yeah, I-I like editing more than writing. But we have the number one newspaper in the country so it's kind of—it's **top-notch**—it's-it's kind of like it would be in real life.

INTERVIEWER: So you think you might like to be a journalist?

HIGH SCHOOL STUDENT: Um, more of an editor 'cause, uh, ⌈journalism . . .⌉

INTERVIEWER: ⌊Why-why-why⌋ an editor instead of a journalist?

HIGH SCHOOL STUDENT: I don't know. I like, I like fixing things more than I like creating them, I guess. Um, it's-it's just more fun for me. I don't, I don't know if I can really explain it.

8. THE ARTIST

Other kinds of jobs—when, um, it's like being an actor, which-which I've also been—you have to do all of these very challenging things, including, in my case, **sheep shearing** was one of them. Uh, I worked—it was a place called the Rurakura Research Station—and I worked on, uh, an experimental sheep farm but you had to understand the, um, the intricacies of rearing sheep and shearing them and all the rest that goes with that business. Uh, and also, um, I mentioned before, but my-my father was a beekeeper and he filled my life with bees, so my childhood was spent surrounded by a swarm of bees; uh, so I've worked at that kind of thing also.

9. THE UNIVERSITY PROFESSOR (ARCHAEOLOGY AND ANTIQUITIES)

UNIVERSITY PROFESSOR: I went to Pompeii first in the mid-1980s and began to study in the excavations there, get some training from some of the archaeologists there, ended up writing my **Ph.D.** dissertation on the architecture of houses in the ancient city of Pompeii, and I've worked there, uh, ever since.

INTERVIEWER: And tell me about the work that you do there.

UNIVERSITY PROFESSOR: Well, I began first by, um, as I say, studying the houses at Pompeii. But, um, there's a lot more to it than just houses. Pompeii is an entire ancient city, uh, preserved by the volcanic material that-that buried it, um, under the eruption of A.D. 79. And, uh, so most of the city has been excavated now. This includes houses, public buildings, all the streets, shops, uh, temples, um, the government buildings of the city are-are brought to light. And so it's a, it's a huge site. You go walk around up and down the streets, go in houses and public buildings and so forth.

When I first went there, I was interested in studying the architecture and I developed a close working relationship with the, uh, superintendent of antiquities, the professional staff there that oversees the site, and so now, uh, that they know me and I have a strong working relationship with them, um, I've been able to, uh, get permission from them to undertake my own excavations. So I go back every summer now, and, uh, I have an ongoing project to excavate and explore, uh, a house that's, uh, commonly called the House of the Large Fountain. It was, uh, it was cleared, uh, first back in the nineteenth century, but it was never properly published and so my project is to document its architectural development and the various phases of the building, excavate underneath the floor to explore, um, periods of habitation that preceded that of the eruption, and then ultimately publish the book in a, publish the house in a detailed book.

10. THE OFFICE MANAGER

OFFICE MANAGER: Um, what we do is we buy things for the university—not for the students, but for the staff, faculty. Um, we buy the equipment that they use; we buy, um, any services that may be needed. We do the contracts for the university.

INTERVIEWER: So what are your main responsibilities?

OFFICE MANAGER: OK, um, I deal primarily with buying **IT** equipment; I do all the contracts for the university, um, the copiers, um, any kind of equipment, that's what I mainly do.

11. THE RETIRED POLICEMAN

RETIRED POLICEMAN: I probably enjoyed the flying more than the, working the road.

INTERVIEWER: Why was that?

RETIRED POLICEMAN: Well, because I felt like I was really helping people with the, with the flying. And I always wanted to fly. And I always wanted to fly helicopters. Now it wasn't, there wasn't a whole lot of pretty sights because most of the people that we transported were in **pretty bad shape** for them to be, uh, transported in a helicopter, so you got to see a lot of, you know, really **messed-up** people physically. But the good part of that was that 85 percent of the people we transported survived because we **got 'em** to a **trauma unit** within that **golden hour concept**, so that was a good thing, and it was really rewarding when you'd be sitting in a hanger **waitin'** for a flight and somebody would walk in and say, "Hey, uh, **y'know**, I just wanted to stop by and thank you for **flying me in** six months ago," y'know. And you start talking to the guy and he tells you the incident and you think, "Wow, I remember this guy, like his leg was just hanging on or whatever," and here he is **walkin'** around. Especially like, um, children. We-we transport a lot of babies, premature babies, and, uh, I remember landing at a **medevac** one night and I shut down because I had to take, you know, pry the person out of the car. And a guy came up with a little kid about six years old. He said, uh, and he remembered me, I didn't remember him. He said, he said, "You remember me?" I said, "No." He said, "Well, you transported my baby when he was premature and took him to the hospital." And I said, "Oh, **how's** things going?" And he said, "There he is." And here's this healthy little kid, y'know, and I said, "Boy, that's amazing," that that guy remembered me from the hospital, and we probably **dealt with** each other for ten minutes, that he saw me, y'know, and flying that helicopter but he remembered that, and that makes you feel good.

12. THE UNIVERSITY PROFESSOR (LINGUISTICS)

INTERVIEWER: So do you have a research specialty?

UNIVERSITY PROFESSOR: I focus on, um, discourse analysis, primarily focused on American Sign Language.

INTERVIEWER: And what sort of things do you investigate specifically related to your research interest?

UNIVERSITY PROFESSOR: Discourse is a pretty broad topic, which means basically looking at how people interact in situations, so how do they tell stories, how do they have conversations, um, and my particular subspecialty then is to, how do people who are having conversations using American Sign Language or telling stories in American Sign Language.

INTERVIEWER: So how did you come to choose this particular arena for your work?

UNIVERSITY PROFESSOR: Um, I think I always was fascinated with how people communicate, and I didn't realize until much later in my life that you could get paid for looking at that. Um, so since I always had this fascination with how people interacted, I always enjoyed getting people to tell stories and looking at, "Oh, well, that was a funny situation. Those two people seemed to be having a great conversation and then one person totally didn't get what he was saying and what happened?" And when I was in college, I came across a course called anthropological linguistics, and I enrolled in that course and was completely fascinated. One of the topics that was sort of a topic of one half of the course was gender communication, and in the reading packet was this reading from this professor at Georgetown University by the name of Deborah Tannen, and I was like so fascinated with this work,

I thought, "This is the greatest! Gosh, I mean if I could go and do something like this all the time, that would be amazing." But—the time—I still didn't grasp that there was a whole field of linguistics we could get into, and so I just sort of put it off, out of my mind, and then in my senior year of college, I enrolled in a course called American Sign Language and then got to thinking and doing some research and realized, "Oh, if I go to D.C., I can focus not only on American Sign Language but also on this discourse component because Georgetown and Gallaudet University are in the same city." And so that's sort of how everything fell into place.

DEFINITIONS

adjunct faculty: People who teach at an educational institution and are not members of the regular faculty but are hired to teach specific courses, usually on a part-time basis.

ALS (Advanced Life Support): A form of temporary life support that is performed on a person who has suffered breathing or cardiac arrest, which includes all the aspects of BLS, plus the administration of medications to help resuscitate the person.

BLS (Basic Life Support): A form of temporary life support that is performed on a person who has suffered breathing or cardiac arrest, part of which is CPR (cardiopulmonary resuscitation).

book the dates: To schedule a time for something.

CPA (Certified Public Accountant): A licensed professional who performs various financial tasks, such as the preparation of tax returns, audits, and accounting, for individuals and companies.

dealt with: To have interacted with or talked with another person.

dialysis: A medical procedure used on persons with kidney failure to cleanse the blood of waste products.

driving a Cadillac: In this context, a phrase that means being rich, financially well-off, or wealthy. (The Cadillac is an American-made luxury car.)

EPA (Environmental Protection Agency): An agency of the U.S. federal government that is responsible for protecting human health and safeguarding the environment.

expantiate: A nonstandard construction used by the speaker. The standard word usually used in this context would be *expand*.

flying me in: To provide transportation by air.

gated community: A group of private residences usually surrounded by a wall, a fence, or another physical barrier, with access controlled by a gate and/or guard.

golden hour concept: The first sixty minutes after a person has been involved in a trauma or serious medical situation during which it is critically important to get him or her to emergency medical care (usually a trauma center) to ensure the person's survival.

a good ten years: At least ten years or definitely ten years.

got 'em: A common colloquial verbal contraction for *got them.*

Great Lakes: A group of five large freshwater lakes in northern Midwestern portions of the United States near the United States–Canadian border.

how's: Contraction of *how is*. In standard English grammar, one would usually say "how are" in this particular context.

HUD (Department of Housing and Urban Development): A U.S. Cabinet department that is responsible for addressing the country's housing needs and urban community development, as well as enforcing fair-housing laws.

IT (Information Technology): Equipment, devices, or infrastructure used for transmitting, storing, or processing electronic data.

medevac (medical evacuation): The immediate transportation, usually by helicopter, of a critically or seriously ill or injured person to emergency medical care.

messed-up: Not right or as it should be. In some kind of disarray. To have made a mistake or an error.

911: The universal telephone number that a person calls in the United States for emergency medical, police, or fire services.

outreach: A proactive kind of action in which one person or organization initiates contact with another person or organization in order to address a particular issue or problem.

part-time: When referring to employment, usually defined as a job that is performed for fewer than forty hours per week.

PCBs (Polychlorinated Biphenyls): Highly toxic organic chemical compounds originally used for insulating and cooling.

Ph.D. (Doctor of Philosophy): The highest earned academic degree awarded by a university.

pops music: Popular music. The more common phrase is *pop music*.

pretty bad shape: Very bad or poor condition.

running smoothly: To be taking place as planned or taking place without problems.

sheep shearing: Cutting the wool off sheep so that it can be made into thread, cloth, and clothing.

There but for the grace of God go I: A colloquial phrase that means "It could have happened to me."

top-notch: Among the best.

trauma unit: A special emergency department at certain hospitals that treats critically ill or injured persons.

waitin': Colloquial pronunciation of *waiting.*

walkin': Colloquial utterance of *walking.*

wasn't: Contraction of *was not.*

what have you: Whatever.

y'know: Colloquial pronunciation of *you know.*

QUESTIONS AND EXERCISES

1. What is the most complicated job described in this chapter and why?

2. What is the most interesting or the most boring job described in this chapter and why?

3. What do these speakers like about their jobs?

4. Describe your job.

5. Write a job description for a job that you would like to have.

6. Describe the job of a friend, coworker, or classmate.

7. Identify three words or phrases in this chapter that are new to you, and write a sentence with each one.

CHAPTER 3

AN AVERAGE DAY

In this chapter, interviewees talk about what they do on a daily basis.

1. THE TRAVEL AGENT

Average day, it's, uh-uh, I mean, it's hard from the morning—my average day, you mean from morning to the night? Yeah, my—I have a eight-year-old son—and my wife leaves early in the morning, so it's like a crazy American morning—get him ready, get yourself ready—and I also have a **Subway** so I let him go to school and then go to my Subway, come here, come travel, and go back home, take care of his homework, dinner, and jump in bed.

2. THE SURGICAL TECHNOLOGIST

Uh, we-we go in and we set up the room for cases, uh, we open all the instruments and, um, set up the room, any equipment that we might need for that particular case, and, uh, then the patient comes in and, um, they get put to sleep and we, um, prep them for the surgery and-and **drape them out**, and then the surgeon comes in and I help him get dressed for the surgery and then, um, uh, hand instruments during the-the surgery—and I have to know how to put everything together and, uh, **y'know**, try and think ahead of what he's **gonna** need for the procedure.

3. THE OFFICE MANAGER

Like, first thing in the morning, what we would do—first thing I do, I should say—is check my **e-mail**; uh, morning time is always the better time for me, um, 'cause in the afternoons I just get **bogged down** with returning phone calls and check, and answering e-mail and everything. I like to do in the morning—if I need to meet with vendors—I like to do that in the morning. I'm a **morning person** more so than an **afternoon person**. Um, we typically check the mail that comes in—it comes in around ten o'clock—and we check that, we disburse it out to the various people for them to do what they have to do, um, then we enter purchase orders if there're purchase orders to be done, we enter those purchase orders. We try to **fax** them out now to the vendors because we've found that if we mail it, it's taking a lot longer and departments keep screaming at us and, you know, wanting this right now, so we try to do all that, fax that out in the mornings. And then, in the afternoons, as I said, you know, answer e-mails, answer, um, messages, and just kind of wind down.

4. THE CHEMIST

I have a lot of meetings because I run those three programs and a couple of smaller ones and there're a lot of individual projects that go on for each, um, program and so the—what's going on with the status, what are our next steps, who do we need to work with outside of the agency, uh, meeting with people outside of the agency—so there are a lot, a lot of meetings during the day, um, and a lot of writing, too. I also do quite a bit of that, in terms of, uh, communicating with other people or **briefing things up**, you know, to the upper management at **EPA**.

5. THE ACADEMIC ADVISOR

ACADEMIC ADVISOR: I usually, I go in the morning. Uh, I get a lot of phone calls from the **student**, if somebody has a problem with, in any class or has a problem with a professor or has a problem in his own life, he can talk to me about it and I can explain to him what he has to do and I always let him know about **the time between here and over there**. Over here, the time is very, very valuable. You have to make sure, if you have a class at two o'clock, you have to be there at two o'clock exactly. If you make it five minutes before, it's OK, but do not late one more minute than that time. And back home, timing is—no value for the times. If you have a class at two, you show up two-fifteen, at two-thirty, it's OK. But over here, when you do that, meaning you **underestimate** the professor, and he will get really upset with you, so I always focus about the time because the value here—timing here is money. And back home, time, it's—you know, you have a lot free times.

INTERVIEWER: Now-now, what students do-do you advise? Do-do you advise students at George Washington or . . . ?

ACADEMIC ADVISOR: No, all over the **States**. I have a student at Harvard University, I have a student at Yale University, I have a student at GW—it's all over the States. A lot of them in **Oregon states**, a lot of them here in, um, in **Ohio states**, uh, Florida, California—it's all over the States.

INTERVIEWER: So they—excuse me—so that you, they call you or how do you communicate with you by ⌈ phone ⌉?

ACADEMIC ADVISOR: ⌊We have⌋ like ten academic advisor, each one taking care, like, one hundred fifty student, and I have two assistant help me for any question or any paper have to written up, so, uh, it's basically a lot, a lot of phone calls plus a lot of—some—paperwork on the side.

6. THE LIBRARIAN

LIBRARIAN: Well, there is no typical day. That's why, that's what I like about the job. Uh, I-I work in an office, I have my own office, um, but every day, other than going to work at the same time, is, uh, is pretty much different. Um, some days I'll be working on a-a written report that I'm preparing for somebody who's asked for a background report on a given subject, and I might spend the whole day working on that, um, using the materials that are available to me. I use a computer, I use the computer to do a lot of research. But I work at a library and we have lots of real materials there available at the library as well and I use those. Other days, I may be spending most of my time on the telephone, talking to people and giving them answers to questions that they need much more quickly than if I were to write something in a report or a memorandum. Um, and it, everything in between, really, can-can happen. I-I-I also spend a lot of time doing **one-on-one** briefings for people in their off, going to, uh, an office and talking to people one-on-one, giving a presentation, responding to questions that people may have, so there's a lot of **face-to-face** interaction as well as talking on the telephone, writing reports, that sort of thing—and it's-it's the variety of that sort of **day-to-day** existence that I really like about the job. Not, no two days are similar.

INTERVIEWER: Do you deal directly with members of Congress, or do you deal more frequently with their staff and personnel?

LIBRARIAN: More frequently with staff people, but I certainly do **deal with** members of Congress as-as well. Sometimes the member themself—he himself or herself—wants to have a personal briefing on a topic 'cause they know the particular questions that they're most interested in. Sometimes members of Congress will call directly, which is always kind of a surprise—you pick up the phone and the person says, "This is Senator **So-and-So**," you know. That's-that's certainly more rare but it does happen. But mostly **dealing with** staff people, and there are hundreds of them at any one time.

7. THE EMT

Some-some days are better than others. They're long, we **get a lot of attitude**, um, the-the only reward is just self-gratification, knowing that you did something good for somebody, usually. Um, but during the course of a day, you know, you don't get a lot of appreciation from the people who you care for, so sometimes the days can be pretty long, but if you got a good team and, um, you-you guys know how to just do your job and just-just have a good time, you-you'll be all right, you know, it-it can be fun.

8. THE NURSE

Typically, especially granted that right now I work in the **emergency room**, so, uh, we come on to the unit and it is busy from when we come on until when we leave. Uh, we try to help people that come in with emergencies and sometimes we see people that are-are not really, uh, do not really require emergency procedures but because people are not certain what their health condition is, so

they will approach us and then we'll guide them back to their primary care physicians. But typically it's a, it's a busy, uh, job, working in an emergency room, as a **registered nurse**.

9. THE PROFESSIONAL MUSICIANS

VIOLINIST: Well, that's another big part of our life that we need to juggle very carefully because just the work part is very physically demanding, so if we have like a three-hour orchestra rehearsal, that's three hours of playing and it's very draining—sometimes it's easy but most of the time it's very draining, physically and mentally. We need to **be all there** to perform well, so, you know, when we have like big concerts or big rehearsals, we need to take it easy during the day. So most of the time, we're very good about always doing our scales and like nice warm-up sessions to like just really always play in tune and be warmed up. Um, when we have easy weeks, um, at work, uh, we definitely like practice more during the day, and that's when we have a chance to like, you know, do more of our personal practicing or **get ahead of our game** and practice all the music that we have coming up for the next couple of weeks at work. So, you know, really, to answer your question, it can be—our practicing—can be anywhere between half an hour and like six hours, depending how much we can afford to, like, tire ourselves out.

HORN PLAYER: It's-it's-it's **gotta** happen every day.

VIOLINIST: Yeah.

HORN PLAYER: Um, I'll occasionally take a day off if I'm really fatigued from a-a heavy day or a heavy week of-of playing something; if I'm doing recording sessions or something like that, it can be very physically demanding and I **just plain** need a rest. But, barring that situation, we do have to practice every single day. Uh, typically I'll-I'll practice from two to three hours a day, um, just-just to keep my playing at the level that it needs to be so that when the phone rings, I can say, "I'll be there and I'll be ready." **Boom.** And-and go.

INTERVIEWER: So you have three types of things you have to practice: you have your own personal technical practice, you have to practice the music that you're going to be playing, and then you have your orchestra or group rehearsals, right?

HORN PLAYER: That's correct. Um, I, the, I call it my-my musical calisthenics. I do it every morning, I have this practice routine that I do that, um, keeps me in physical shape so that I can play, uh, accurately, with a good tone, um, and play, you know, the high notes, which takes a little more strength, and low notes, which takes more flexibility. And that's, um, it's a very, it's a very physical thing that we do. Um, a-a-a friend of mine, uh, from the, uh, ski slopes—I do skiing in the wintertime—and we got to talking about small talk, and she asked what I do and I said, "Oh, I'm a musician; I-I play in-in orchestras in the area." And she said, "Oh, you're a classicist!" And I kind of snorted and I said, "I'm not a classicist; I'm a **horn jock**!" you know. It's-it's my job to-to stay in shape, um, it's-it's really, it's a very physical thing. It's like a football player, y'know, doing jumping jacks and stretching and running five miles. You know, you might only see the-the game, y'know, two hours worth of football on Monday night on-on TV but ev—, you can be sure that every member of that team has gone running that morning, they have a stretching routine that they do, they've spent an hour or so studying the **playbook** in the afternoon—it's a very similar thing that we do. So we have a practice session that just keeps us basically in physical and mental shape, and then we'll have maybe another practice session where we learn the notes that we have to play in whatever rehearsal or concert that we're doing—that would be like the football player studying the playbook—and then we actually have either the rehearsal or the performance with the group, which is equivalent to the football player either going to practice with his teammates or playing the actual game on TV on Monday night. Uh, so there are a couple of different levels, a couple of different phases of-of practicing that we do on a regular basis, on a daily basis.

DEFINITIONS

be all there: To be totally prepared or ready.

bogged down: To become overwhelmingly immersed in something.

boom: An interjection that means "There!" or "Now!" or "Then!" or "At that instant."

briefing things up: To report or inform your superior about a particular matter.

day-to-day: From one day to the next day; a usual occurrence.

deal with, dealing with: To interact/interacting with in some way.

drape them out: A part of preparing a patient for surgery: the patient is covered except for the area on which the surgeon is going to operate.

e-mail (electronic mail): Printed matter that is transmitted electronically.

emergency room: The department of a hospital that provides urgent care to seriously ill or injured persons, now more frequently referred to as the emergency department in many places.

EPA (Environmental Protection Agency): An agency of the U.S. federal government that is responsible for protecting human health and safeguarding the environment.

face-to-face: To actually meet with someone in person.

fax (facsimile): The transmission of printed matter by telephone.

get ahead of our game: To go beyond where one needs to be, or to become more prepared than is usually necessary.

get a lot of attitude: A colloquial phrase that means "to receive an expression of resentment, arrogance, anger, impatience, disrespect, or entitlement from someone when it is not appropriate."

gonna: Going to.

gotta: Common verbal utterance of *got to*, which means the same as *have to*.

horn jock: Slang for a musician who plays a horn. (*Jock* is slang for an *athlete*.)

just plain: A colloquialism that means "simply this way" or "exactly this way" or "exactly that way."

morning person (or afternoon person): An expression for someone who feels more alert or active in the morning (or in the afternoon).

Ohio states: Ohio, the state of Ohio [this speaker's usage].

one-on-one: A meeting or an interaction involving two people.

Oregon states: Oregon, the state of Oregon [this speaker's usage].

playbook: A list of plays (strategies) that a player has to learn for his or her sport. This term is most frequently associated with American football.

registered nurse: A licensed medical professional who usually provides patient care under the direction of a physician.

So-and-So: An indefinite term usually used to refer to a nonspecific person.

States: The United States of America.

student: *Students* in standard usage.

Subway: A fast-food chain that specializes in submarine sandwiches.

the time between here and over there: The difference in the way people value time in the United States compared to other countries.

underestimate: To assess or estimate the value, worth, or capacity of something as less than what it is. Nonstandard usage in which the speaker uses it to mean "disrespect."

y'know: Common colloquial pronunciation of *you know.*

QUESTIONS AND EXERCISES

1. Summarize the average day of two speakers.

2. Which day seems the hardest and why?

3. Which day seems the easiest and why?

4. Compare your average day to that of some of the speakers. In what ways is your day the same or different?

5. Describe the average day of a friend, classmate, or coworker.

6. Identify three words or phrases in this chapter that are new to you, and write a sentence with each one.

CHAPTER 4

LOOKING FOR WORK

In this chapter, interviewees talk about how people look for work.

1. THE SIGN LANGUAGE INTERPRETER

Well, the deaf community here in America is a very small community and, um, as well there aren't many men in the, in the profession working as interpreters, and so once the word gets out that you are a qualified, you're a certified professional, uh, pretty much, work finds you. And if you have a level of proficiency in sign language, a level of proficially, proficiency, rather, in interpreting, um, **word**

of mouth has been very helpful. Uh, in terms of finding work, initially I-I lived in New Jersey and I was working, uh, with the courts as an interpreter, and so a lot of the work that I received as an interpreter was through word of mouth, through referrals and also through a state listing. Moving to the area, I also connected with the local courts that were here, it's—a lot of times, in terms of finding work—it's a matter of networking with the community and also a matter of being on a list or two, um, in order to receive opportunities or **leads** for work.

2. THE PROFESSIONAL MUSICIANS

HORN PLAYER: It's challenging. There are a lot of people that are trying to get hired for a small number of jobs. Uh, traditionally, uh, orchestras will hold auditions for any vacancies that they might have, but, of course, there has to be a vacancy first and they'll hold an audition, and depending on the orchestra, there may be anywhere from ten to a hundred people auditioning for one position. Um, now that's the-the traditional way of auditioning and getting a job. Uh, we do **freelance** work, which is a little bit different from that. Um, a lot of the jobs that we do, uh, will last like a-a week, and then we move on to something else. I-I tell people that it's kind of like being a plumber—you know, once you go and fix somebody's toilet, then you go on to the next house the next day or the next week. Um, and for freelance-type work, um, uh, we are both members of the musicians' union, uh, and that's one way to get known. The musicians' union in this area has what's called a showcase audition where members of the union can play, uh, a very abbreviated audition in front of the orchestra contractors in the area and you pass out your résumé, and if they like the way you play,

then they'll hire you for these short-term jobs. Uh, but really, probably more importantly than that, it's just, uh, reputation. You get to know people, um, you know, you **show up** on one job, you play well, um, and, uh, hopefully your name gets out amongst the people that are-are, uh, hiring musicians and, uh, we also get referrals from other musicians. A lot of my work comes from my other, uh, horn-playing colleagues. They might get asked to do a job and they say, "Well, I'm not available that weekend, but you should call Paul 'cause he's good-good player and-and reliable."

VIOLINIST: Yeah, I mean, you pretty much covered it all. I guess another way also to find work sometimes is to take the-the big auditions that are announced in the area and you know, you may not win the spot but every orchestra, good or, I mean, good or bad, big or small, they all have **sub** lists so, uh, that's another good way to, like, find work, is to, like, for as many contractors or as many orchestras you can and even sometimes when you don't win the job, you still get a lot of work out of it because there are always people that are sick.

INTERVIEWER: What's a sub list?

VIOLINIST: A sub list is, um, a list of musicians that are in a certain order depending how good they are—and basically, let's say, uh, one violinist in the Baltimore Symphony Orchestra is sick at the last minute, then they need to fill that spot for the week, so they will, like, get their violin sub list out and call violinists and, you know, depending how well you did on an audition, you can be number one or you can be number fifteen, so you can . . .

INTERVIEWER: And what's the hardest thing about finding work in your field?

VIOLINIST: O-of, the hardest thing . . .

HORN PLAYER: Um, I guess for freelance work, it **just plain** takes time. It-it takes a long period of time for your name to get out there, and it takes a lot of persistence. Um, uh, so the hardest part about getting work when you're first getting established is just not getting discouraged, uh, because the work is-is very intermittent at first. But as your-your reputation gets more broadly known, uh, then you start to work more consistently and-and hopefully with better and better jobs, uh, jobs with better orchestras, uh, better paying jobs, um, uh, as-as Lysiane said, we do different things every week: we might be doing an opera one week, we might be doing, um, you know, I might be doing a wedding with my brass quintet the next week, uh, so you have to be very flexible, and um, uh . . .

VIOLINIST: Well, I guess in a way it's like we're not finding work. We have to like basically announce ourself and wait for the work to come to us so it's, there's always, like, a lot of expectation, and we're kind of, like, waiting for the phone to ring. So I guess what's really hard—**one of the thing** I find the hardest is, we always have to be **on top of our game**. So, you know, the phone can ring now and I'm asked to, like, go play a big concert tomorrow so, you know, if I haven't touched my violin in a week and I'm not **on top of my technique**, you know, I'm not **gonna** go play well at that **gig** tomorrow, and that's the last time that contractor will call me. So, that's **one of the big challenge**.

HORN PLAYER: Yeah.

VIOLINIST: Is that we always, you know, have to be right there, ready to play if we want to, like, if we want to keep having good work.

HORN PLAYER: Yeah. Ano-another big challenge is juggling different jobs. For instance, um, I-I-I'm—just this-this week—I've gotten asked to do a couple of good jobs in-in the Baltimore area that I had to turn down because I had already made a commitment to another job which was not so good but as-as I said, our reputation is critically important, so if you have a reputation of backing out on jobs at the last minute, you're not gonna continue to get called for stuff, so once you make a commitment, it's very important that you **honor it** even if-if you're losing money by turning down other-other potential jobs. That's a very frustrating part of it. You wish that you could take this job and move it to this week and that job and move it to this other week so that you can fit everything in, but obviously it-it doesn't work that way.

3. THE MECHANIC

INTERVIEWER: How did you get this job?

MECHANIC: Well, it took a long process of working at other mechanic shops, Jiffy Lube, uh, working at my dad's shop, working on cars, and I got here, uh, just for a paycheck for right now.

INTERVIEWER: So you've always had an interest in cars
⎡and things like that⎤?

MECHANIC: ⎣   Yeah,   ⎦ mos-mostly in transportation, due to the fact that people always need to travel or go somewhere so they need their car to count on.

4. THE ENTREPRENEUR

ENTREPRENEUR: I've found that in hiring and firing of people, that you're not going to hire someone and train them to be **customer service**–oriented. A person is either like that on their own or they're not. And I've actually hired people for jobs that were less qualified for the job **technically speaking** because their **people skills** greatly outweighed it. And I've found over the years that the person that has the better people skills is more valuable to the business, regardless if their technical skills are somewhat lacking.

INTERVIEWER: You find it easier to train them technically than to train them interpersonally?

ENTREPRENEUR: Yes, yes. You can have the best tattoo artist in the world, but if he's unable to communicate with the customer, he's not gonna do very well for himself or the shop; same with the **tandem master**, same with the pilot. Now, if you have a guy who is mediocre abilities but is able to appease the customer on his own, he-he will gratefully accept your contributions to him learning his **technical ability**, where the guy who already has the technical ability and knows he's good, has a little bit of **an attitude or an ego,** he's not willing to listen to your criticisms about his customer service skills.

5. THE **CPA** AND THE **IT** PROFESSIONAL

INTERVIEWER: What do you think is the hardest thing about finding work in your respective fields?

CPA: Competing with other people. I mean, just, you know, it's-it's a competition. Uh, you know, you-you have to have something that the, you have to offer something that the other person doesn't and that's, you know, in my line, that's why education is very important and to be able to have that piece of paper that—it stinks that you have to have a piece of paper to prove that you know something where there's a lot of people that don't have the paper that actually know more, but, **y'know**, that's just not how the business world is.

IT PROFESSIONAL: Right. You generally have to have, you-you have to be able to back up the fact that you have this education, right? And if you have that education, um, and then you go in and you conduct yourself in a manner that's gonna, y'know, show these people that you can do the job, that's really what they're looking for. I think they're more so looking for that confidence factor and the fact that you-you have some knowledge of it, capacity to learn. These are the common—that's the most common—trait.

INTERVIEWER: What's, I mean, what's the hardest thing about finding an IT job at this point?

IT PROFESSIONAL: Um, well, there's not too much 'cause there—you—anyone in IT will tell ya, "Oh yeah, go look for a job, you'll get four offers tomorrow." You-you get, I mean, for me, at least, and this—I've only been with the current company for a year—I generally stay at computer companies a lot longer than most IT people. They say in that industry that you should move around a little bit, to expand your horizons and see different systems and see how they interact and work and that's generally, uh, a good **rule of thumb**, but I actually have a little bit of security in the fact that I am with the company for longer than many other employees and I can do the job. So, a lot of employers like the fact that—my other computer job, I stayed at with for five years, which is pretty long time at one company, and if they see that, they know that there's some loyalty there—they may be more, you know, apt to go with, go with that.

6. THE TRAVEL AGENT

Oh, when I came to America, I, uh, I came alone and, uh, it-it was very hard to find any kind of job. I was national manager for a travel agency in India, so I thought that it's-it's like America is like a **five-star hotel** of the world so you can go and walk in, you can make lot of money on any kind of job, but that was not true. I, no one would, no one would give me a job because nothing—no school, no college—and so I could practically go to a grocery store and do a job of **filling the aisles**. But I-I kept looking. Eventually I found a job in New York, and, uh, a wholesaler of a travel agency, uh, airline travel, and they—he—agreed to pay and give me a job which was for, uh, a-a money which I can't even say it—and naturally, it was—to get a job in America was very, very difficult. You go, and it's, you can get the minimum pay jobs, but it's—to get on—it's like a very strong, uh, **glass ceiling** for-for me and, uh. So eventually I decided that I'm-I-I worked in a-a-a national travel agency called Liberty Travel and, uh, and they-they agreed because I worked for almost four years here in America—that's how they gave me a job and it was a minimum paying job. Then eventually, when I knew that I have to take care of my son, his education, his college, everything, I need more money, so I had to start my business and, uh, thankfully, the country is such that I could make it, I could make it, yeah.

Uh, we have people go on the website, **Subway**, they can file their application from there, they can come to the store and file the application. And when I think I need somebody—I mean, the application doesn't say anything—when I interview people, I try to see how, uh, people-friendly they are, are they, are they, ever worked in a fast-food industry or if they have the attitude to-to, uh, to fit in-in a team. And once I have that then I give them two days, without employing them, I pay them for two days and I let them go through the training with me for two days. And if during those two days of training—which is not enough—but I think at least in those two days of training, I see the potential, whether they are willing to learn, if they are willing to perform. Sometimes, if somebody is, uh, not able to, then I just simply say, "Would you still like to continue? It's a hard job for you." And, uh, I have, uh, I mean, I have people with a difficult family background so they also see that they have family to take care yet they need some money, so . . . It-it's difficult but it's interesting.

DEFINITIONS

an attitude or an ego: A negative or inappropriate, arrogant, pompous, or self-centered disposition.

CPA (Certified Public Accountant): A licensed professional who performs various financial tasks, such as the preparation of tax returns, audits, and accounting, for individuals and companies.

customer service: In business, addressing and meeting the needs of the customers or clients.

filling the aisles: Usually stated as "filling the shelves" or "stocking the shelves": putting merchandise on the shelves in stores so that it is available for customers to see and purchase.

five-star hotel: The finest, most luxurious kind of hotel. Hotels are often rated on a scale of one to five stars, with five stars being the best possible rating a hotel can receive.

freelance: Employment in which the person finds his or her own work and goes from job to job without a long-term work schedule.

gig: A term, frequently used by musicians, that means "job" or "performance."

glass ceiling: In an organization, a position of advancement that can be seen or perceived but cannot be attained for various reasons, most of which have nothing to do with the person's actual skills or qualifications for the position, such as gender, race, nationality, or ethnicity.

gonna: Going to.

honor it: To fulfill a commitment. To do something that one said or promised he or she would do.

IT (Information Technology): Equipment, devices, or infrastructure used for transmitting, storing, or processing electronic data.

just plain: A colloquialism that means "simply this way" or "exactly this way" or "exactly that way."

leads: Information that provides an opportunity to achieve, or a direction toward, a given end or objective.

one of the big challenge: Usually "one of the big challenges."

one of the thing: Usually "one of the things."

on top of my technique: To be sharp, well prepared. To have a skill that is well developed.

on top of our game: To be well prepared.

people skills: Traits or abilities used in working with people.

rule of thumb: A common or generally accepted guideline or way of doing something.

show up: To appear or be present at an appointed place.

sub: A portion of a larger entity.

Subway: A fast-food chain that specializes in submarine sandwiches.

tandem master: A professional skydiver who is qualified to take another person on a skydive in which that person is attached to the tandem master, and the tandem master is responsible for controlling the skydive and operating the equipment.

technical ability: Specific skills and/or knowledge needed to perform a given job or task.

technically speaking: Refers to addressing the technical aspects of a subject.

word of mouth: Information passed from one person to another through conversation or the direct contact of one person with another person.

y'know: Colloquial pronunciation of *you know.*

QUESTIONS AND EXERCISES

1. List four or five ways that these speakers found work.

2. Explain what was hard or easy about finding work for these speakers.

3. Which job was the easiest or the hardest to find and why?

4. How did you find your current job?

5. Describe how a friend or coworker found his or her job.

6. How would you tell someone to find a job?

7. Identify three words or phrases in this chapter that are new to you, and write a sentence with each one.

CHAPTER 5

INTERVIEWING FOR A JOB

In this chapter, interviewees talk about various aspects of interviewing for jobs.

1. THE HOTEL MANAGER

Absolutely, absolutely I learn a lot. Before you go to the interview, you have to know what you are going to do, you have to know, uh, you expecting, what type of questions going to ask, you have to get some idea about the job before you start to interview, and you have to have a good résumé, a good written résumé about the job. At the same time, you have to be on time, you have to be—look—nice, uh, you have to know how talk with the people, you have to know how to explain to the director what you are going to do, and so forth. And this comes from experience. I did a lot of interviews, and you learn from one and another, so I learn a lot from interviews.

I did hire a lot of people and, uh, and one of, uh, I can't say, it's really—I couldn't catch it up with one Indian guy, he was applying for a job, he was very, very nice guy and, uh, he's very strong and, uh, he knew what he doing but he can't talk, but I didn't know that. And he has his cousin with him and every time I ask him question, his cousin answer the question; the other guy, he just keep looking to me. But this is one of the—you know, I learned af—, later on. I didn't fire this guy. He was my friend and I let him get the job and then I let him work 'cause he's a hard-work man. But he doesn't, you know, I don't want to say handicapped, but he can't communicate. But every time I ask him question, his cousin answer that, answer, you know, the question, and I just keep ask-asking question and he keep answer. And when I put him on the floor to do the job, he do it excellent, so there's no reason to **fire him**; I hire him. And I keep him and I let him work, and he do the job and he was very successful, you know, and, uh, I like people get the job done, that's my point, to get the job done. At the same time, I treat him **like a family**, I always sit with them. But there is a line between management and employee, you have to keep the line all the time, don't get close, don't socialize, just keep the line 'cause I learned the hard way. . . .

Basically, you got to know about the job, whatever. Are you going to work in the kitchen as a cook? You have to know how to cook. 'Cause I hire people in the kitchen—I have people in the, in the, in the food and all the food and beverages—the big, uh, big department. So if you're working as a cook, for example, you have to know how to cook, you have to have some experience, you have to have a good résumé. At the same times, I have to **check him up**, I have to call at least two or three places he used to work before and, uh, check his references, check his background. I don't hire people right away. So I learn a lot how to interview, how to follow up an interview. After I check his references and I, uh, I give him the chance to start working and—very important—that show up on time, very important you got to be very clean, very important you wash your hand, there's a lot of stuff to make sure, uh, everything you produce, uh, how you say—everything to give to the client, make sure it's very nice and clean and healthy. So if you're using your hand, you have to have gloves, everywhere you go you have to have gloves, you know, you don't touch anything, don't touch any food with your hand, and so forth. So, uh, like I said before, you have to get some experience about the job. At the same time, I give him the chance to work, and if he start working and **he do excellent job**, I keep him but if, you know, if doesn't do his job, so, with, uh, executive chef, we can decide both of us to let him go.

2. THE ACCOUNTANT

ACCOUNTANT: Uh, that was, I guess, while ago, um, but now I'm more on the other side of the interviews, I'm the one hiring, uh, but, uh, my interview was, um, what was it like? It's, you're in a little room with, like, three other people, and they ask you a bunch of questions. Uh, I've always, uh, I've always tried on **both ends of interviews** to, uh, just to keep it very normal and conversational, uh, and to get a sense of the person and make sure they get a sense of me, uh, rather than trying to give any sort of prepared answers or draw out any prepared answers from, uh, interviewees.

INTERVIEWER: How would you suggest that a person prepare for a job interview?

ACCOUNTANT: My-my biggest thing is that I want them to have done a little bit of research, know who we are and what we do before you come, get online, find the website, read through it, see what we do, uh, my **bio**'s there, read my bio, that kind of thing. Um, just come with some understanding of the business and, um, other than that, I, you know, it's a—the field is—what-what I do in public accounting, there's a technical aspect to it, but it's also a lot of interpersonal so that you have to get a sense of both, um, and an interview can flop either way where they can, you know, sometimes interviewing somebody, if I get a sense of what their technical skills are but you don't have an idea of them as a person, then I haven't learned what I need to know, um, so again I try to keep it semiconversational and get them **off-topic**.

INTERVIEWER: So what do you think makes a good job interview, from, uh, the perspective of employees' point of view—or from your point of view?

ACCOUNTANT: I think a lot of it is **body language** and just being comfortable and you look for those things, to see whether they're fidgeting. Um, I had one person that brought her **pocketbook**, and the whole time in the interview, she's got her pocketbook and she didn't put it down, so she's **messin'** with it the whole time and that's— you're not **gonna** win in that setting, um, when you do those sort of things—but it's, you know, some measure of polish, uh, but also just a-a level of comfort, uh, the, because the idea is—and I'm sure you've heard this—but the idea is, you know, we don't just want to hire you to do the work we assign you, we want to hire y—, we want to find someone we want to work with every day. So it's both of those things.

The ones that are really good are the ones that don't feel like an interview. Um, when afterwards, if the person just sort of comes and we realize that we just sort of talked with them for a while and left with, you know, that feeling that you know the person can do the work and you **wanna**—wouldn't mind—if they were in the office all the time, um, that's a really successful interview.

3. THE UNIVERSITY PROFESSOR (FOREIGN LANGUAGES)

UNIVERSITY PROFESSOR: Well, I teach at Gallaudet University, which is a university for deaf students, and I'm a linguist but I teach in the Foreign Languages Department, so I actually teach Spanish and sometimes I also teach courses that have to do with linguistics, too: **sociolinguistics**—or topics related to linguistic issues.

Uh, from the perspective of the interviewee or . . . ? Um, well, I think if you get to connect with the people that are interviewing you who are, obviously, the people that you're gonna be working with, I think that makes for a good interview because I think that you have to be yourself. I mean, you can't go to an interview pretending to be someone else or pretending to know something that you don't know, and if you are yourself and you're honest about what you can do, what you can't do, then it's important to really connect with the people that are interviewing you, uh, so that they'll-they'll get that you're being honest and that, uh, and that you'll be a good person to work with.

INTERVIEWER: How should somebody dress for an interview?

UNIVERSITY PROFESSOR: Well, I guess it depends on the job. Uh, academic jobs tend to be, um, uh, people tend to dress casually for-for academic jobs so, you know, for a, for a teaching job, I would never dress too formally—I mean, I, it, you give the wrong message. Uh, being part of a community means sharing certain values and, uh, if you show up in a suit with a tie, you might give the impression that you're too **square** or too conservative or that you're trying to pretend to be someone that you're not, so I think that might actually, uh, give the wrong impression, so for, like, a teaching job, I would dress, you know, well but casually. Uh, for another type of job, for a business job, I would, you know, I assume people would dress more formally, but I've never had that kind of an interview so I've never had to worry about that.

4. THE SIGN LANGUAGE INTERPRETER

Well, in general, if you want to prepare for an interview, you have to know a little bit about the company that you're looking to work at and so, we have the Internet, we have, uh, the library as well—people sometimes forget the library—but just doing whatever research is necessary to find out about the company, to find about the history, to find out as much as you can about the, um, officers of the organization and that industry or the field that they're working in. After you get that basic information, it's just a matter of sometimes just practicing, a matter of going over your experiences and seeing what, uh, match you can provide to the company, based on your **skill set** that you bring to the company.

5. THE **IT** PROFESSIONAL

Um, the job interview. It was probably the first time in years that I put on a full suit, in at least five years. I actually dressed up in a full suit. It was, uh, the-the atmosphere is, y'know, more **corporate America**, it's commonly known as corporate America, and, uh, the offices are very nice, mainly cubicles, uh, but, uh, you basically act and conduct yourself in a professional manner. So I decided, "I don't want to put on the suit; I'm gonna put on the suit for the other people, just because other people like it."

The interview lasted approximately four hours, which I thought was pretty long. Uh, it was probably one of the longest interviews I've been on. I met with three different people. I met with, uh, the head of the IT Department. I met with technical lead, uh, and two different technical leads of two different I—, part of IT. Um, they—the head of IT—just wanted to see if I could conduct myself in a professional manner, didn't really ask me any technical questions, that's what I was most worried about, and even the technical people didn't even ask me that. I offered more technical information to them than they had really expected, and they thought that I would clearly be able to do the job. Um, I think in an interview situation like that, I meet the, if I meet the, uh, the head of IT and he's a real friendly guy, uh, first thing I'm gonna do is stand up, shake his hand, and say, "Hey, how's it going, **bud**? I know we, you know, miscommunicated sometimes on some phone calls and, you know, but finally we did it, you know, great to meet you." And that's actually how our— my—interview did start when I did meet this guy. And that just **puts everything at ease**. He's easier to talk to, um, he-he knows I, you know, I'm out there, I'm, I want this and-and I did. You know, when you're going for a job like that, it's—I didn't—a lot of people are forced into a cer-certain scenario or job that they don't necessarily care for or are not, don't necessarily, have that drive to get. Um, I feel lucky, in fact, that this is sort of something that I wanted to do. Uh, when I go out there and, you know, meet with these people, I'm like, "Yeah, bring me on board!" Uh, you know and I'm-I'm gonna do it. I, one of the-the points that I made very clear during my interview is, y'know, if there is something that I don't know how to do, I'm **(a)** gonna learn it, **(b)** gonna ask somebody how to do it, or **(c)** research it myself somewhere on the Internet and make sure it gets done.

6. THE NURSE

There's three key things with me: your skill level, for what you are, what the position you're applying for. You have to be able to, uh, do the things which you—is required of—you. Now if you go above and beyond, that's a plus, but I expect the standard and basic things that an **EMT** or, for example, a registered nurse should be able to do. Secondly, your presentation. You could be as skilled as possible but you do not approach the public well or the

clientele or the customer well. You have to be able to present yourself and represent the company. And thirdly, respect to everybody around you, your coworkers. So, skill level, presentation, and respect. To me, those are key. It covers—sort of embodies—everything. If you can respect your coworker, you should treat them properly. You don't have to be super nice to them, you just have to be polite and courteous to them, as well as the public.

7. THE CPA

CPA: I was eighteen. I was finished school but hadn't officially graduated yet, and my teacher called me and said, "Hey, this company called us; they asked me to send my two best students to interview, so I'm calling you." And, they said, you know, "It's out on York Road," and I was like, "OK, you know, I'll give the lady a call." So I gave the lady a call, her name was Rose Ward, and she happened to go to the same high school I did, about twenty-five years earlier, had the same teacher I had, about twenty-five years earlier. So I thought that was very interesting. But as she and I talked, we had an immediate connection over the telephone, so she asked to come in, you know, for this interview. So I was like, "OK," you know. She, "When can you come in?" I was like, "Well, whenever-whenever you want me to!" You know, kid ener-energetic. She was like, "Well, can you be here by two?" I was like, "Sure, I can be there by two!" I didn't drive, never had a car. I'm thinking, but, you know, "I can, I can **pull this off**." So I did what all young girls do—I called my dad. "Dad, can you leave work and take me to this, you know, to this job interview?" And he had a pretty flexible job, so he was like, "Sure, you know, I can, I can get **ya**." So I was like, "OK."

So then I'm thinking, "OK, next hurdle: what do I wear?" I didn't have any business clothes, and this was an office, you know. So, I went up in my mom's closet and I found a skirt—she was a little heavier than I am, so I sewed it down the side quickly to make it fit—and threw-threw on the jacket and stole some of her pantyhose out of her, you know, cl—, um, drawer and, you know, went on the interview.

The interview lasted about four hours, which I wasn't expecting. I interviewed with every person in the organization, it seemed like. I interviewed with the lady, Rose, first, and then I **hadda** fill out the actual application, and then I hadda go for a typing test, which typing really wasn't my **strong suit** but, you know, we got through it, and then I met with, um, the personnel manager, and I sat with him it seemed like just for hours and I brought with me my little résumé that we hadda make in school— that was part of our assignments—and so I had my int—, that, and then I had different type of certificates from volunteer work and being on the honor roll and different accomplishments so I had this little portfolio of myself. So I had this interview and I was just, you know, **nervous to death** and then—my dad's, of course, out in the parking lot, waiting for me, it was **pouring down rain**, so I'm thinking, "Oh, my poor dad," you know. And so finally it ended, and he was fine. I'm like, and, you know, he was like, "That's what happens." And that was my . . .

INTERVIEWER: And you got hired?

CPA: I was, it took a few weeks. Like, I-I, um, I wrote a letter, a letter of thank-you afterwards—like they teach you in school you're supposed to do—and made follow-up phone calls, you know, like, while we're—they're—still waiting for the other person to come and interview who then never showed up and, you know, then finally they were like, "OK, we'll just hire you," you know, because it was like they were tired of waiting for find, to-to find, somebody else. So I was like, "Ooh, yeah, that's good!"

DEFINITIONS

(a), (b), (c): A common way that speakers list items they are describing.

bio: Short for *biography*; a summary of a person's life or work history.

body language: The way a person moves or positions his or her body in an interpersonal situation, from which people often infer information about what the person is actually thinking or feeling.

both ends of interviews: Being both an interviewer and an interviewee.

bud: Short for *buddy*, an informal term of address usually used between men.

check him up (check him out): In this context, to investigate someone's background.

corporate America: A reference to the American business world or culture.

EMT (Emergency Medical Technician): An allied health professional who is responsible for responding to medical emergencies and providing initial first-aid care and transportation of the sick or injured persons to a medical facility.

fire him (fire): To terminate a person from employment.

gonna: Going to.

hadda: Colloquial pronunciation of *had to*.

he do excellent job: In standard English grammar, *he does an excellent job.*

IT (Information Technology): Equipment, devices, or infrastructure used for transmitting, storing, or processing electronic data.

like a family: Usually *like family,* meaning to treat a person the same way one would treat a member of his or her own family.

messin': Messing.

nervous to death: Extremely nervous.

off-topic: A subject in a conversation, discussion, or meeting that is different from the main subject of interest.

pocketbook: An older term for a woman's purse.

pouring down rain: Raining very hard or heavily.

pull this off: To do something or accomplish something, often when there is some uncertainty about the outcome.

puts everything at ease: Creates a relaxed or comfortable atmosphere or feeling.

skill set: A group of skills relevant to a particular job or task.

sociolinguistics: A field of linguistics (the study of language) that focuses on the intersection of language forms and social interaction.

square: Very conventional in outlook, dress, attitude, and/or behavior. Rigid or out of touch with conventional or current social norms.

strong suit: The thing at which a person is most skilled or does best. (This term comes from the card game bridge. It is the suit for which the person has the most cards.)

wanna: Want to.

ya: You.

QUESTIONS AND EXERCISES

1. What is the purpose of a job interview, according to these speakers?

2. List what these speakers see as the most important parts of a job interview.

3. How should you prepare for an interview?

4. Describe your last job interview.

5. Describe the last job interview of a friend, coworker, or classmate.

6. How should you dress for an interview?

7. Identify three words or phrases in this chapter that are new to you, and write a sentence with each one.

CHAPTER 6

TRAINING FOR A JOB

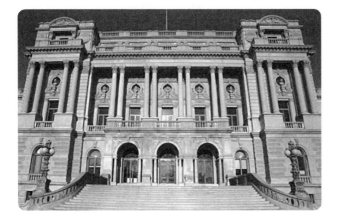

In this chapter, interviewees talk about what kind of training they have had for their jobs.

1. THE LIBRARIAN

Well, I went to college. Um, I attended the University of Michigan, and my studies at the University of Michigan were in journalism. I started out thinking I wanted to work in newspapers or maybe advertising or something like that. Um, then my career took several turns over the years and I ended up here in Washington—I'd grown up and gone to school in the **Midwest**—um, and it turned out that the journalism background that I had is very useful no matter where-where you go. And where I am now, the ability to communicate clearly and succinctly to members of Congress who don't have a lot of time to absorb the information that they need, that's a very useful skill that I have. So I-I continue to use the journalism even though I'm not, strictly speaking, working in journalism now. But I, then I also went to graduate school and got grad—, got a graduate degree in environmental studies, and that was where I sort of merged the journalism and the, uh, and the environmental interest.

2. THE UNIVERSITY PROFESSOR (LINGUISTICS)

UNIVERSITY PROFESSOR: I teach linguistics here at Gallaudet University, um, specialize in language acquisition of children, first language acquisition. So how children, um, go between the ages of one to five, they seem to pretty much get down all the grammar of the language that they're exposed to and that there's mistakes that they make along the way but surprisingly few. Um, my specialty is children who are exposed to and learning **American Sign Language** as a first language, although this year I've started working with children who are bilingual, who are exposed to both American Sign Language and English, just to see whether their development looks different from that of monolingual English or monolingual **ASL** learners.

I-I didn't really have the normal training I think that most people in this field have. I went through biology and French as **my undergraduate** and then graduated with that and decided that I'd like to go into linguistics, so started graduate school in linguistics. Um, I happened to work for a woman whose research project was the acquisition of ASL, so that's how I sort of fell into it and got my training along the way, um, so I guess normally it would be nicer to have an undergraduate in linguistics but that wasn't always available, so . . .

INTERVIEWER: Did you find the transition, how did you find the transition?

UNIVERSITY PROFESSOR: Oh, very awkward. It was, uh, I think that I-I was naive going into linguistics thinking that since I loved languages and they were easy to learn that, uh, linguistics would just be a lifelong career of learning lots of languages and having the excuse to do it as much as I wanted. Um, I was getting away from biology because I felt like it was too analytical and there was too much memorization and too much theory. It turned out that there was actually a lot more of that in linguistics than in biology so, um, I fell right back into a theoretical field but it still has to do with languages, it still maintains—retains—some of that pleasure of learning languages and being exposed to languages and having the excuse of doing it as your job, so it wasn't as bad as it could have been.

3. THE **EMT**

EMT: Uh, EMT course is a, is a simple course, relatively; it's a sixteen-week course, it's, you go to school about maybe two days a week, four hours a day. So, for someone who was interested in the **EMS** field, it would be really good because they-they don't have to really have a—long—periods of time in classrooms or long training periods. It's just a lot of reading involved and a lot of information just about, you know, various aspects of the body, just the systemic systems and just what to do for

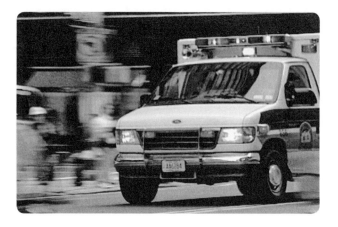

'em, what you need to do. So basically as an EMT, my-my thought of it is, whatever your situation is, **I gotchu**. You know, it doesn't matter—if you got a headache, I gotchu; if it's a gunshot, I gotchu; **diabetic crisis**, I gotchu; if you just lonely and don't feel good, I gotchu. That's the EMS state of mind.

INTERVIEWER: Do you have to take additional training and education?

EMT: I have to do, um, **continued medical education**. Every two years, we're required to take a **refresher course** and to accumulate **CME** credits throughout the years. I've also been trained as a **medic**, um, since then, which was another additional year of schooling but now is a collegiate program, which is a two-year program now, um, so you-you have to continue-continuously study. One thing about the medical field—when you take this as a career, you accept the fact that you're a student for life. As long as you're in this field, you will have to learn, you—because things change every few years—so you have to keep up with new curriculum, new technology so you're-you're a student for life in this.

4. THE SIGN LANGUAGE TEACHER

[Interpreter: What kind of training do you have to teach ASL—your skills, certification?]

I do have a certification, Ameri—, from the American Sign Language Teachers Association. You have to go through their courses, fill out a form, an application form, how many hours you have of teaching experience and your methodology, how you would teach certain subjects, aspects of your curriculum—that's all on the application form—and then they send you a certificate. You start with a provisional certificate and then after you have some experience with that, then you take an exam that they send you—they have several questions on the exam such as how do you evaluate your students' **signing** abilities, things like that, so you would explain that and send that back to them. They'll look it over and, uh, three evaluators look that over and if all of them feel that you're qualified, then you get another certificate, but your goal is to move up to the top level, which is a professional certificate. And right now I'm in the graduate program in linguistics, and I feel like that will really benefit me, uh, for the professional certificate because I'll be able to analyze the language a lot better and that will help me with, uh, getting up to the professional certificate. That along with my experience teaching here at Gallaudet.

5. THE SIGN LANGUAGE INTERPRETER

Well, there's always the importance of having a basic education, uh, in terms of high school. I went to, uh, high school in New Jersey, and I went to a **vocational-technical high school** initially that was focusing on technical electricity, and I still **dabble** with electricity on the side. Um, after completing school, I didn't immediately go to college; I started off working for an insurance company for about seven years and later went back to school. I went to, uh, an adult college at first, Thomas Edison State College in New Jersey, and a lot of the experience at that college was working on portfolios and demonstrating life experience to receive credit for college-level work that you have. Um, after that, I attended, uh, New York University for graduate school—I have a master's degree in deafness rehabilitation and along the way, uh, I became interested in sign language—this is somewhere between high school and attending college.

6. THE CHEMIST

CHEMIST: Well, I actually have a doctorate in organic chemistry, and I started off at **EPA** as a chemist, but I knew before I went to EPA that I wanted to start doing more policy work so, um, while I was finishing up, I took some econ-economic classes, too. So I started off doing chemistry and then I moved into melding my scientific background with, uh, doing more policy issues, and it's been pretty interesting and it's very useful at an organization like EPA, having a strong scientific background.

INTERVIEWER: Why is that?

CHEMIST: Um, because you really understand the issues and there are a wide range of scientific issues and it's, y-you have enough of a grounding in science, let's say with chemistry to understand the toxicology, which is really important at EPA, some of the environmental, uh, science—and I think it's much easier to learn the policy aspects than for a policy person to learn the scientific aspects, so. And it's a good sort of, uh, balance to be able to work in both worlds and to work with both scientists and with the lawyers and the other policy people because they do think differently, and you end up being a bridge between the two. It's-it's quite interesting.

7. THE OFFICE MANAGER

OFFICE MANAGER: Typically, what we needed, we need, is a bachelor's degree—um, you can substitute that for experience—and then you just learn on the job, that's what it was. For instance, my bachelor's is in Spanish and French. I haven't used that in—as a matter of fact—since I've graduated. So, um, and you don't need Spanish and French to-to purchase so, um, just a matter of learning . . . you know . . .

INTERVIEWER: On the job.

OFFICE MANAGER: On the job, on-the-job training.

8. THE ENTREPRENEUR

ENTREPRENEUR: Uh, all self-taught. I graduated from high school and other than that, I have no formal education. Um, I studied other successful businesspeople in the United States, uh, bought some tape programs and audiovisual tools, and, uh, just followed their footsteps.

INTERVIEWER: What about learning how to run a skydiving school?

ENTREPRENEUR: Same thing. I went somewhere, took some skydiving lessons, became a skydiver myself, then, uh, bought a couple airplanes, and hired some people that were already rated and knew how to instruct people and basically learned from them over the years how to obtain all the ratings.

INTERVIEWER: Do you repair the airplane yourself?

ENTREPRENEUR: Yes, I do.

INTERVIEWER: So how did you learn to do that?

ENTREPRENEUR: Uh, when I was a kid, my father was a maintenance man at a factory—pretzel factory—and he could fix everything, and I kinda just learned from him. And I think it's more of an attitude than a skill, the mindset that there's nothing I'm unable to do, eliminate the word *can't* from your vocabulary, and believe you have the power to find the information to create the knowledge to accomplish whatever needs to be done.

9. THE MECHANIC

INTERVIEWER: What kind of training or education did you need for this job?

MECHANIC: Um, I had to go to two classes, um, one on tires, learning what tires, um, more of like the tires that, uh, sizes, the meanings, um, what type of tires are right for this vehicle or not. And the other class was just like an orientation, saying, "These are your days off, um, **these're** your benefits, which you get after you work so long, and you get raises so many times a year."

INTERVIEWER: How long did the training class for learning the tires ⌈last⌉?

MECHANIC: ⌊Six⌋ hours. I mean, it was just a long class and afterwards, we just sat down and watched a video. We, uh, showed the instructor that we can change tires and balance 'em and repair 'em.

INTERVIEWER: And then, during-during your training process, when you start working, are you supervised or do you have a **probationary period** or do you . . . ?

MECHANIC: Yeah, we have a ninety-day probationary period, which, um, we're just looked over after, um, just-just make sure we do everything right the first time so we can be set off on our own.

DEFINITIONS

American Sign Language (ASL): A form of manual communication used by deaf and hard of hearing people in the United States. ASL is an autonomous linguistic system structurally independent from English. It is different from sign languages used in other countries, such as Italian Sign Language or Japanese Sign Language.

continued medical education (CME): Additional education required in some medical fields beyond the basic education that is required to enter the field. This additional education is necessary in order to stay aware of new information and changes in a given field.

dabble: To do something or participate in something in a less-than-serious or fully committed way.

diabetic crisis: A medical emergency caused by too much or too little blood sugar in a person's body.

'em: Common shortened pronunciation of *them*.

EMS (Emergency Medical Service): A field of health care that focuses on providing emergency medical care to sick or injured individuals. The term *EMS* is usually used in reference to those who first respond to an accident or a crisis (first responders), such as EMTs or paramedics.

EMT (Emergency Medical Technician): An allied health professional who is responsible for responding to medical emergencies and providing initial first-aid care and transportation of the sick or injured persons to a medical facility.

EPA (Environmental Protection Agency): An agency of the U.S. federal government that is responsible for protecting human health and safeguarding the environment.

I gotchu: In standard speech, *I got you*. A colloquialism that means "I'll take care of you" or "I understand what you mean."

medic: See **EMT**. This can be short for *paramedic*. A paramedic is similar to an EMT, but with additional education and training. The term *medic* is often used in the military to refer to a person, similar to an EMT or paramedic, trained to give medical assistance in battlefield or combat situations.

Midwest: A term used to refer to the central portion of the United States.

my undergraduate: Here, the speaker means her majors (fields of concentration or specialization) in college.

probationary period: In the employment world, some predefined period of time at the beginning of a person's employment during which the person has to demonstrate that he or she can do the job for which he or she was hired.

refresher course: A course designed to update a person's knowledge of a particular subject.

signing: The use of sign language.

these're: Contraction of *these are*.

vocational-technical high school: A kind of second-ary educational facility that specializes in teaching skills and crafts that will facilitate helping the student obtain employment in some kind of trade, such as carpentry, auto mechanics, welding, plumbing, or electricity.

QUESTIONS AND EXERCISES

1. What kind of training do these speakers have?

2. Which job requires the most training and why?

3. In which jobs does the training relate directly to the work?

4. Describe the training required for your job.

5. Describe the training that was required for a friend's job.

6. What kind of on-the-job training have you had?

7. Identify three words or phrases in this chapter that are new to you, and write a sentence with each one.

CHAPTER 7

COMMUNICATION AT WORK

In this chapter, interviewees talk about communication issues they encounter at work.

1. THE UNIVERSITY ADMINISTRATOR

Well, I work here at Gallaudet University. Uh, right now, I'm the special assistant to the president and that's been for a couple of months. Before that, I was a professor of education, teacher training.

Meetings in my life? Well, they start about, what, seven o'clock in the morning? Uh, I mean, I have meetings every day with the president of the university. Those are the meetings where I do the listening. I meet with other people where I get to talk more or **sign**. Uh, because of some of the things that the university is going through right now, there's a lot of listening and listening for messages that are not the spoken or the signed messages, but they're the messages that, **reading between the lines**, the feelings that people are expressing but not saying. So a lot of my meetings are, uh, for both of us, therapeutic.

2. THE ACCOUNTANT

Meetings? Uh, we don't really do a lot of meetings. Um, I know other work environments do. In public accounting, a lot of it is working on your own or in a small team. Uh, there are meetings with clients, and those are either formal or informal, but those are useful because if they're in a meeting setting, they kind of have to answer your questions and-and make some progress. Meetings in our own office are not, we don't have a lot of formal meetings, uh, and I think what meetings we do have tend to be more of the **team building**, um, than any kind of useful thing. Everything now is, you know, you figure it out by **e-mail** or some informal thing in the hallway rather than in meetings.

In a first client meeting, uh, we **wanna** make sure— our main thing is to get—we have to understand how their accounting system works, uh, a brief understanding of who **the players** are and who does what, um, who has access to the system, **whatta** they do. Uh, the biggest thing for what I do is finding out where the problems are, what are they trying to get us to achieve. Uh, so it's, you have to understand the system and then what they want to see happen. Uh, and it could be, uh, I'm not getting the kind of reports that are useful or it could be, uh, I'm not getting them when I need them, or, you know, it's these kinds of things but you j— have to find out from them, uh, what they're looking for which is often not necessarily easy to find out. They don't often know what they want you to do, they just know there's a problem, and it's not working, uh, but that's-that's the meeting, uh, in the beginning.

In those settings—and this is for if a group is already a client—it's the first meeting with, you know, they've-they've signed an agreement, right? Uh, it's a little bit of an interview where you're asking them questions but **the point** of it is really to get them to talk. Uh, we don't necessarily have specific things; you have some specific things you need to learn, but it's more the more they talk, the more likely it is that they'll **stumble upon** what it is that's really bothering them that led them to call you in the first place.

3. THE ENTREPRENEUR AND THE SURGICAL TECHNOLOGIST

ENTREPRENEUR: Everyone, from all walks of life, all nationalities, race, creeds, and colors, a variety of products and services that I offer entails just about every walk of life. And, uh, in those dealings, you need to be a **chameleon**— I think has helped me. When someone walks in my tattoo shop with a suit and a tie on, I address them in a different fashion as I do the guy who pulls up on his motorcycle. And the same here with the skydiving. And I think it's the same in communication when you're speaking with someone. I find myself usually tending to speak very fast because I want to get my point across quickly and don't want people to have to wait, but some people have a hard time perceiving or getting your meaning because you're going too fast, and I find myself—you have to slow down when you're talking to that person. And then, on other occasions, if you're in a slow or relaxed or tired state and your story or conversation is **dragging on**, I can sense the person on the receiving end is getting **antsy** and they want me to step up the pace of the conversation a little bit. I think that's very important when you're communicating with someone, is to present the information to the person in the best way that they're able to receive it.

We go out and we're disappointed with **customer service**—and I guess it's because we're not in the customer serv—, well, we are, every—, we believe everyone's in the customer service industry and-and I think—and some universities have done studies, as you're probably well aware—that your ability to climb the **corporate ladder** in your job and career is more to do with your ability to deal with people, whether they're above you, below you, the customer, the client, uh, your boss, your subordinate, et cetera.

INTERVIEWER: Uh-huh.

ENTREPRENEUR: And we, we both do the same thing, you know. We're trying to see how much humor does the person need to have, how much serious do they need to have, should we talk fast, should we talk slow, should we use little words, big words, to give the person whatever they need to make them feel comfortable. And our jobs are very-very different but we both basically do the same thing.

SURGICAL TECHNOLOGIST: When you go out and someone has a customer service job, we-we both get very upset when you know . . .

ENTREPRENEUR: You walk in and their only job is to stand behind the counter and help you and they're unable to perform that task.

SURGICAL TECHNOLOGIST: You walk in, they don't even look at you or they don't acknowledge you or say, "Hello, I'll be right with you." You know, it-it gets both of us very upset.

ENTREPRENEUR: Yeah, that's interesting.

INTERVIEWER: Because you're frequently, very—I mean, on a daily basis—on the, you're on the other side of that.

ENTREPRENEUR: Yeah, well, my job is to take you to jump out of an airplane or to fix the airplane or to give you a tattoo or to pierce your body. Her job is to, you know, help the surgeons to fix your body, but yet we're both very well **in tune with** giving everyone around us what they need to make them happy and comfortable. So, when we go to a restaurant and the waiter's only job is to make us happy, they don't have to prepare the food or wash the dishes or clean the table, **all's** they have to do is make us happy. If they're unable to do that, it's very disappointing and it makes for an unpleasant experience. And then we find ourselves usually not going back to a place like that. And I think that's one attribute to my success of all my businesses—I've always worked very hard to make sure everybody is happy and content and gets what they need, outside of the product and the service.

INTERVIEWER: Do you, in situations like that, do you say something or do you just **let it go**?

ENTREPRENEUR: Just let it go. We don't wanna . . .

INTERVIEWER: Seen it before.

ENTREPRENEUR: Yeah, we don't want to **cause no stink**.

4. THE **IT** PROFESSIONAL

IT PROFESSIONAL: Customer service—we're in a world nowadays—is growing devoid of customer service. And I think that when people realize that they can sit down, pick up the phone nowadays, the **land line** and talk to you to get an answer, that actually is tremendously beneficial nowadays. Even people in IT—my supervisor, who is five years younger than me, has said, "Oh, I tell you, people in these e-mails drivin' me nuts!" Because it can be, it's-it's—sometimes it's overkill—it becomes overwhelming, you know, and he-he's-he has more technical skills than I do and he says, "**Y'know**, just-just give me a call, y'know, just give me a call, so much easier, I can talk to you about it." And it's, and it's a little more entertaining. We-we get tired of the monitor after eight hours and when you have a good level of communication and a good level of customer service and you can talk to these people and they **sorta** understand what you're going through, even so, if, even if you have a bad day, you might be able to explain it to a person and then get an extra day of work involved.

INTERVIEWER: Uh-huh.

ENTREPRENEUR: So, that's—those things—I think are imperative.

5. THE TRAVEL AGENT

I mean, it's a, dealing with public is **pretty interesting**. That, uh, most of the time, uh, my energy goes into trying to understand the temperament of that person. And, uh, once I understand and I feel comfortable about it, that I know that this person cares about, uh, what am I giving you, because, by the, by the way, what I give, any other travel agent will also give. I mean, it's the same cruise ship, it's the same cabin, it's the same bed, so what am I adding? It's only—my evaluation is—it's the service I can provide or I understand where-where their fears are, what they like, what they don't like, so put everything into perspective. If somebody says, "I-I heard that when you go to cruise, you come back **adding weight**." So I know that the person's, uh, basic concern is weight, or "Do I have to eat or do I have to go to every dinner or do I have to do this or I'm trapped if I have to do anything else?" So I need to explain that it's not just the food on cruise; there's entertainment, I mean, there is, there-there-there are clubs, you can go for exercise, so I need to talk from the perspective of health, cruise, healthy cruise, so. Uh, it's pretty interesting to-to understand how, uh, how people react to the same thing, which is vacation, and, uh, it makes me—it makes it—more interesting because I-I come from India, and, uh, I have not studied in America, I have not gone to college or in any school in America, so for me to understand American culture, it, the-the-the local day-to-day jokes **doesn't come to me that easy**, so I n—, I-I need to understand that.

6. THE SURGICAL TECHNOLOGIST AND THE ENTREPRENEUR

SURGICAL TECHNOLOGIST: I deal with the community, so everybody that makes up our community, which can be pretty wide range of people. Uh, and the hard part for us is, it's sort of similar to what you said, some people come in, they're nervous, they need you to joke around and make them relaxed; other people come in, they don't want to see you joking around, it makes them nervous and think that you're incompetent, so you have, you have to get a feeling for the person and the patient and what-what they're **gonna** need from you.

ENTREPRENEUR: That's a good elaboration on what I was saying, and I find the exact same thing, you know. And-and say when you're conversing with someone, some people want you to joke around and be humorous and be funny and other people want things to be . . .

SURGICAL TECHNOLOGIST: ⎡Professional.⎤

ENTREPRENEUR: ⎣ Logical ⎦ and literal.

SURGICAL TECHNOLOGIST: Yeah.

INTERVIEWER: Uh-huh. And-and you see people at a very difficult time in their lives.

SURGICAL TECHNOLOGIST: Yes. They're-they're nervous, they're-they're worried, and, you know, they-they need some support from us and . . .

ENTREPRENEUR: This is interesting. I think in essence, this part of our job is the same 'cause when someone's getting a part of their body pierced or a tattoo or jumping out of an airplane, it's a very dramatic part in their life and they need you to be this person who she's describing to you. Some people need to see super professional, serious and other people need to see lighthearted humor or some variation of those. That's interesting.

SURGICAL TECHNOLOGIST: And we want them to feel comfortable so they'll come back to our hospital and you know, we can be a community hospital, so . . .

ENTREPRENEUR: And we want them to come back because we want their money.

7. THE RETIRED POLICEMAN

RETIRED POLICEMAN: It was some pretty rugged training when I went through the police academy, and I'm sure that was to prepare you for dealing with the public. And the problem with the police department is, most of your—you know, they say in business, the customer is always right? Well, in our business, mostly the customer was always wrong, so they weren't too happy about, you know, you stopping them and, uh.

But I-I was lucky when I got out of the police academy, you-you got to ride with, uh, a experienced trooper, and I was fortunate enough to get a guy who really had a lot of **street smarts** and common sense and one of the first things he taught me was, when you stop somebody or you're dealing with somebody, just imagine that you're in his shoes and what kind of, what kind of action would you like taken against you, you know. And he said, "You have a lot of power with that badge. Don't abuse it."

And I **took that to heart** and I st—, I think to this day that that probably kept me out of more *trouble*. And by trouble I mean going into a bar fight or whatever. I-I got into very few physical confrontations where I actually had to do something. A lot of people threatened you but he, and there again, he taught me, you know, you, most

people you can reason with. And if you go in with an attitude and he's got an **attitude**, there's gonna be a fight. So
you have to defuse the situation, try to see his point of
view, if-if he has a legitimate point of view. And one thing
that comes to mind, I remember a truck driver delivered
some product to a-a business in Annapolis and he was
supposed to be paid at the time he made the delivery and
the guy didn't—wasn't gonna pay him—but he wanted
him to drop the product, which was a boat, I believe. So
they got into an argument and he pulled out a **tire iron**.
And the guy was probably my size, about, outweighed me
by a hundred pounds at least. And this guy was upset. So
I get there, so he, you know, I step out of the police car,
here's a Maryland state trooper standing in front of him,
so now he thinks that the guy that doesn't want to pay
him has called me so now I'm gonna team up with that
guy to nail him. So he's standing there with a tire iron.
And I looked at 'im and I thought, "This guy can cause a
lot of problems." So I, first I got, I stayed away from him,
I didn't get too close to him, and I said, "Tell me the situation." So the businessman explained his part and-and
then the truck driver explained his part. He said, "This is
what I was told to do," and he said, "I'm not leaving here
without the boat." And I, so-so I told him, I said, "Well,
I think this guy has a legitimate gripe"—the-the truck
driver. And I could see him relaxing then, you know, and
then finally I said, "You know, what you need to do is put
the tire iron down," I said. "There's-there's not gonna be
any need for that, nobody's gonna get hurt here." And
after about twenty minutes we got it calmed down and
the guy got in his truck and left with the boat and the
business owner had to call the company and say, "Hey,
well, I'm gonna make other arrangements," but he just
thought he was gonna strong-arm this guy. Had I walked
in there with an attitude, probably both of us would have

been laying on the ground with a big dent in our heads from that tire iron.

INTERVIEWER: Mmm.

RETIRED POLICEMAN: And I saw other police officers who would approach that situation like that with a-an attitude and they always got into trouble. We had one trooper that I worked with, he was constantly calling for help, and all because of his attitude.

8. THE CHEMIST

CHEMIST: Uh, some of them, people are briefing me, so they'll come in, they'll have sent up a-a briefing paper, the briefing paper will have background, will lay out the issues, uh, will present options, uh, often a recommendation, uh, so I need to make a decision and it either gets raised up one level or it'll just get implemented after the decision. Sometimes, uh, briefing my, uh, direct boss on an issue that has been run through me with, or my staff and so, you know, and we discuss the issue, implications on other parts of the agency, that's, you know, the higher, the higher you **brief up** or you go up, the broader the look is across an organization. Um, sometimes we meet with, uh, folks from other agencies, um, **NGOs**, sometime, um, with industry, sometimes with other countries because of the international work with, um, with mercury. So it really is, it's a lot of meetings and a lot of . . . and I'm-I tend to be an introvert so, you know, at the end of the day, it's, "Let-let me write a document," you know, stay in my office and write and catch up, catch up with my e-mail and . . .

INTERVIEWER: Are you—in these meetings—are you in-in charge of the turn taking and communication and, or-or it depends?

CHEMIST: I think it-it depends. So, um, I-I don't think they're very formalized in a lot of meetings, um, I don't run a lot of, uh, more basic mee—, I don't mean more basic meetings, but when you're doing the initial analysis, when you really do need the **turn taking**, that's really important. The-the meetings that I'm mostly at, somebody will be going through a document or an issue and then other people will say, "Well," you know, "let me add this or let me add that," but it's often the person who's doing the briefing and whoever is the decision maker where there's the most interaction.

9. THE SIGN LANGUAGE TEACHER

INTERVIEWER: Do you have—as part of your teaching—do you have to have meetings with, uh, other teachers or with your supervisor and what, what are, what are the meetings like?

TEACHER: Yes, I-I had, I recently had another meeting with an **ASL** teacher here and at the beginning of the semester we all get together and talk about the best approach, the best methodology to use for teaching, what kind of evaluations we give, what kind of exams. We have, we see examples of good tests and bad tests and discuss the pros and cons of each, um. We also discuss policies for ASL teachers, like, for example, if one teacher is sick, how do you go about getting a **sub** for that class. Also, one of my favorite things is how to teach **classifiers** in ASL, so we discuss that and each—we **brainstorm** different ideas for how to teach that, based on our experiences. Also, if there's some problems with students, how to handle that as well.

DEFINITIONS

adding weight: Usually expressed as *gaining weight* or *having gained weight*.

all's (all): A colloquialism that is a contraction of *all is*.

antsy: Slang for *restless, nervous*.

ASL (American Sign Language): A form of manual communication used by deaf and hard of hearing people in the United States. ASL is an autonomous linguistic system structurally independent from English. It is different from sign languages used in other countries, such as Italian Sign Language or Japanese Sign Language.

attitude: In this context, a preconceived idea or disposition, usually negative.

brainstorm: To say or present ideas as they are thought of or as they come to mind.

brief up: To give a briefing or report to superiors.

cause no stink (usually **cause a stink**)**:** To create a disturbance or disruption.

chameleon: A kind of lizard that can change its color to match its surroundings; also used to mean a person who is able to readily adapt to his or her surroundings or different situations.

classifiers: Signs used in American Sign Language to show the movement, location, or appearance of an entity.

corporate ladder: Metaphor for the path that leads to promotion and advancement in the business world.

customer service: In business, addressing and meeting the needs of the customers or clients.

doesn't come to me that easy: There are some things that the speaker doesn't understand immediately.

dragging on: Continuing for an extended period of time in a less-than-desirable way.

e-mail: Electronic communication sent over the Internet or local computer networks. (Often compared with snail mail, which is regular paper communication sent through the postal system.)

gonna: Going to.

in tune with: Being aware of another person's needs or feelings; empathetic.

IT (Information Technology): Equipment, devices, or infrastructure used for transmitting, storing, or processing electronic data.

land line: A telephone connection made over a wired network instead of a wireless one.

let it go: To dismiss or ignore something without taking any action concerning the situation or what happened.

NGO: Nongovernmental organization.

the players: In this case, the phrase means "the participants." It does not mean members of a sports team or competition.

the point: The purpose or the objective.

pretty interesting: Very interesting.

reading between the lines: Inferring meaning or obtaining information from something that is said or written beyond the literal meaning of the message.

sign: To use sign language.

sorta: A common colloquial pronunciation of *sort of.*

street smarts: Education (not formal), knowledge, and awareness that come from experience or living or "being on the street."

stumble upon: To find or to become aware of something by chance or by accident, rather than intentionally or by design.

sub: Substitution; substitute (here, a substitute teacher).

team building: A process of developing camaraderie and cooperation among people who work together.

tire iron (or lug wrench): A tool used to remove the nuts that hold a tire on a vehicle.

took that to heart: To have taken something very seriously and remembered it to use as a point of reference or guiding principle.

turn taking: Exchanging opportunities to talk, one person after another.

wanna: Want to.

whatta (or whadda): Slang for *what do.*

y'know: Colloquial pronunciation of *you know.*

QUESTIONS AND EXERCISES

1. Which jobs require a lot of meetings?

2. Which jobs require the most interaction with the public?

3. In which jobs is customer service important and why?

4. What kind of communication is required for your job?

5. What is meant by customer service?

6. Describe a good and a bad customer service experience that you have had.

7. Identify three words or phrases in this chapter that are new to you, and write a sentence with each one.

CHAPTER 8

DRESSING FOR WORK

In this chapter, interviewees talk about what kind of clothes they wear to work.

1. THE LIBRARIAN

LIBRARIAN: Well, I wear professional business dress, um . . .

INTERVIEWER: Is there a **dress code**?

LIBRARIAN: Not, not specifically but I always try to be dressed in a, in a suit, perhaps, or, um, some, certainly not casual clothes at all. Um, even if I think I'm going to be sitting in my own office working all day, I never really know that that's the case because I could get a call in the middle of the day saying, "Can you come over in half an hour to talk to the senator or the congressman about **such and such**?" and I don't want to be wearing **casual Friday** kind of clothes, uh, on an occasion like that.

2. THE ACCOUNTANT

It's—the **dress**—has really changed. Uh, when I started just ten years ago—at a different firm, I was in Baltimore—uh, you had to wear a suit and tie every day, uh, in the office, uh, because what we do is, we're-we're in the office some of the time and at client sites some of the time. Uh, in the office now, it's, you know, it's **business casual**, so it's slacks and a shirt. Uh, and on Fridays, you can pay five dollars to give to charity and wear jeans, so it's really **eased up**. Uh, but coming up, you had to wear a suit every day in the office.

The other side of it is when you're at clients, you have to mirror . . . uh, the guideline we always tell people is you **mirror what the client does** and just **take it up one little notch**. Uh, the first day you're at a client, you always, you al—, I always wear a tie. Um, but, uh, a lot of our clients—we do a lot of work with **nonprofits** in **D.C.**—in a lot of nonprofits in D.C. are, they're, it's not that formal a work environment, they don't want to see you coming in in a suit and tie every day, um, so, uh, you have to mirror that a little bit but, but step it up a tiny bit.

3. THE SIGN LANGUAGE INTERPRETER

Depends on where I'm working. I—as a, as a sign language interpreter—I'm in a number of different settings. Uh, oftentimes, thinking back on my experiences in New York, I was on **Wall Street** and so, of course, that would mean a suit and tie. Uh, if I'm in court working as an interpreter, suit and tie, because the appearance, your-your dress should **mirror the environment** you're in. Uh, I also work in medical settings and so, if it's in surgery, for example, one day you're in scrubs, which is something quite different. Um, I've also done Broadway shows—I'm working on a show right now, a Broadway show, *The Color Purple*, to interpret, and it's probably going to depend on what the people on stage are wearing. And so, the dress, it changes according to the environment that you're in, and so pretty much, what I do is, the night before, I look and see where I'm headed the next day and just try to find something to wear that would correspond with the setting that I'm going to be in the following day.

4. THE **IT** PROFESSIONAL

IT PROFESSIONAL: For this interview, I was obviously clean shaven, wore a full suit, tucked-up **goatee** just so that I personally don't want to have somebody judging me for something that may look out of **corporate America**. They may not be like that and in, for instance, uh, now, since I have the job, I could get away with wearing this probably five days a week. I don't think anyone would say anything. And in th—, IT industry, it's a little more lenient. Obviously, the computer world's changed quite a bit and, uh, you know, companies like Google allow you to wear **flip-flops** or have many different things, uh, going on. And our company's not quite like that but it's sort of lenient in the IT department. ⎡ I guess . . . ⎤

INTERVIEWER: ⎣ So you wear ⎦ business casual to work?

IT PROFESSIONAL: Business casual, I wear business ⎡casual . . .⎤

INTERVIEWER: ⎣You don't⎦ wear a suit to work?

IT PROFESSIONAL: I do not wear a suit and since I've started there, I've not worn a tie, once. I've, I wore a suit to interview in and a tie, and you know, full-full suit to interview in, and I have not worn anything but a **button-down shirt** and maybe some khaki casual pants.

5. THE SURGICAL TECHNOLOGIST

SURGICAL TECHNOLOGIST: Well, I'm lucky: I can wear whatever I want in and then I change into **scrubs**, uh, at work, so I-I don't have to have any work clothes, which is nice.

INTERVIEWER: Does the hospital pay for your scrubs or do you have to buy **'em**?

SURGICAL TECHNOLOGIST: They, no, they-they supply 'em and they wash 'em and so we go in, we put the scrubs on, and then, uh, at the end of the day, you take 'em off and there'll be another pair for **ya**.

6. THE MECHANIC

INTERVIEWER: What kind of clothes do you wear in the course of your job?

MECHANIC: I mean just-just the uniform, a shop uniform with a dark blue/black pants and black shoes, boots type things, just to make sure your feet are comfortable.

INTERVIEWER: Are there, uh, are there things you shouldn't wear to work, in terms of comfort or safety or . . . ?

MECHANIC: Um, I guess street clothes is something you shouldn't wear **'cause** they just get dirty too quick. And jewelry is another thing that you shouldn't wear, 'cause, like, if you touch a car battery with a ring and touch the other part with your car—or the other part of the car—it will actually weld the ring on the battery.

INTERVIEWER: I guess you've seen that happen to a few people.

MECHANIC: Uh, my dad's friend, it happened to him once, and he had a burn mark all the way around his ring finger.

INTERVIEWER: So, do you have to buy your own work clothes?

MECHANIC: No. They're supplied to us; we get two weeks worth of clothes. We wear them one week while the other week, they're being washed.

INTERVIEWER: Do you have to wash them or does the company wash them?

MECHANIC: Um, I tend to **wash 'em** myself due to the fact that they charge twelve dollars to wash 'em.

INTERVIEWER: You save a little money.

MECHANIC: Just a little.

DEFINITIONS

business casual: Dress attire that is not completely formal, but not totally casual. For men, this usually means a dress shirt and slacks (but not a coat and tie or a suit). For women this usually means a blouse and slacks, blouse and skirt, or an average dress (but not a suit).

button-down shirt: A dress shirt, specifically one on which the tips of the collar are buttoned down.

casual Friday: In some organizations, a policy that allows employees to dress informally on Friday.

'cause: Common shortened pronunciation of *because*.

corporate America: A reference to the American business world or culture.

D.C.: District of Columbia. Short for *Washington, D.C.*, the capital of the United States.

dress: In this context, the kind of clothes that people wear, not specifically a woman's garment.

dress code: Guidelines for how someone should dress or what kind of clothes a person should wear in a given place or situation.

eased up: Became more relaxed or less strict.

'em: Common shortened pronunciation of *them*.

flip-flops: A sandal-type of footwear.

goatee: A short, often pointed beard covering only the chin.

IT (Information Technology): Equipment, devices, or infrastructure used for transmitting, storing, or processing electronic data.

mirror the environment: To dress or behave in a manner that is appropriate for a given situation.

mirror what the client does: To do what the client does, or behave and dress as the client does.

nonprofits: Companies that do not attempt to make money (profits) from what they do.

scrubs: Lightweight clothing often worn by medical personnel, usually in a hospital setting.

such and such: An indefinite term usually used to refer to a nonspecific thing or topic.

take it up one little notch (often **take it up a notch**): A slang expression that means "to improve a little," "to make a little more of an effort," or "to increase in intensity a little."

Wall Street: The main financial district of New York City, often used to signify the American business and/or financial world as a whole.

wash 'em: Common pronunciation of *wash them*.

ya: You.

QUESTIONS AND EXERCISES

1. Describe the dress required for each job mentioned.

2. What is meant by casual Friday?

3. In what ways do these speakers think dress is important?

4. How do you dress for your job?

5. Is dress important for your job? Why?

6. What are the consequences of not dressing appropriately?

7. Identify three words or phrases in this chapter that are new to you, and write a sentence with each one.

CHAPTER 9

PROBLEMS AT WORK

In this chapter, interviewees talk about different kinds of problems they encounter at work.

1. THE NURSE

NURSE: Patients or staff?

INTERVIEWER: Let's start with the patients and then we can go to the staff.

NURSE: With, uh, with patients, uh, predominantly, uh, sometimes, uh, they expect more than we give them

because, uh, they will come with multiple, uh, issues. If, for example, you come, we have, uh, to prioritize care—airway, breathing, circulation—and if you come and we realize that, for example, you fell and bumped your head and there was a little **nub**, we do an x-ray, a **CAT scan**, and it's negative and we can, uh, at this point tell you almost with certainty that you're gonna be OK, go take some **painkillers** like Motrin and you'll be fine and don't probably require more care, and so. There's also situations where, uh, some patients come and they do not have, uh, **primary care physicians** and the tendency of the **emergency room** is to take care of the emergency and send you back to somebody that is, uh, supposedly, uh, who supposedly knows you better, like your primary care physicians. And in most instances, if they do not have it, they would want more care, uh, administered to them to take care of this problem, so—in other words—uh, they come into the emergency room and expect a one hundred percent, uh, **wholistic care**, and emergency rooms, uh, usually do not provide that, unfortunately.

INTERVIEWER: Do you ever have other problems with patient dissatisfaction beyond that, in terms of, you know, behavior or any issues like that in the emergency room?

NURSE: Uh, dissatisfaction usually stems from the wait period, because you wake up at three in the morning, for example, and you have a serious bellyache and you come to the emergency room and the waiting room is packed and full, sometimes the wait period could be three, four, to six hours, it's not **unheard of**. And so, if this is a true emergency, where it's a life and death situation, it doesn't matter what we do after a long wait period, you already have a wall between the patient and the care administrator. So, uh, once they have to wait too long, they become impatient and, uh, as a result, uh, they will feel, for example, that we did not give them our best care. And also sometimes, uh, it's hard to please everybody all the time, so maybe we'd **fall short** on certain instances, uh, and so there's dissatisfaction, it happens.

INTERVIEWER: So what sort of problems, if any, do you encounter with the staff or coworkers?

NURSE: Delegation problems, predominantly. Uh, the echelon of, uh, health care practice, you have the physician who is at the top and, of course, the nurses and then other practitioners like respiratory care, uh, physical therapy, and then the nursing assistants, and so on. So sometimes there's not a clear communication of roles and distinctions so sometimes there's friction when you delegate some, uh, responsibilities.

INTERVIEWER: So how are those sorts of problems resolved?

NURSE: Usually, uh, if-if it is, uh, team, the **team approach**—which is a, to my mind, the better approach—uh, you try to, uh, solve this problem over a period of time. It's not a, uh, **one-stone kill** solution, uh, because you try to communicate with these people so that if it happened on Tuesday, you take time out and talk to them and try to regulate it so that on Wednesday and Thursday, it does not repeat itself. So you sort of, uh, follow it, uh, through sequentially so that it's resolved more than just a one-stone kill solution.

INTERVIEWER: Do you find that that approach is successful?

NURSE: Most often than not. And then, on other occasions, uh, it is sometimes people's **work ethic** or work attitude that, uh, is very unchangeable and, uh, inflexible. In situations like that, you have to take it to a-another level, which is probably reporting it to the charge nurse or a superior, uh, person in the echelon.

2. THE RETIRED POLICEMAN

Hmm, well, police departments are—I'm sure when you watch the news, you hear about police departments and you hear about **crooked** police officers and crooked judges and crooked lawyers and I can tell you that's all true. It's-it happens. I didn't see so much of it in the state police, although with, uh, like local police departments. And not that the state police didn't have a few people that did that kind of stuff. And you-you would be approached by maybe another police officer or a lawyer or whatever to do something about a case, and I think every police officer gets to a point where he can go—there's a **fork in the road**—you can do it right or you can **bend to the will** of these people and-and when you do that, then they, you know, they've got something on you, so. And when I got to that point, I said, "Not **gonna** happen." And I got into a lot of trouble, and by *trouble*, I mean, uh, where other police officers wouldn't talk to me because I wasn't one of the-the gang, you know, I-I wouldn't cooperate and I **told 'em**. I said, "That's—I'm sorry—that's the way it goes. I don't care who the person is. They're-they're not above the law." And in a way, it worked out for the better, because I didn't get as many promotions when I worked the road and I wanted to fly, and if **I'da** been too high in rank, I wouldn't have been able to fly, so I figure it worked out for the better. So that was the only, I just avoided those people, you know—lawyers—I just avoided them if they called me up, I said, "I really have nothing to discuss." But for the most part, I'd say 99 percent of the people I dealt with in the state police were **on the up and up**. Just a very small percentage that were political.

3. THE TRAVEL AGENT

Uh, problems, uh, happen—it's more technical, it's something like somebody booked a ticket and, uh, airline, after b—, taking the money canceled their flights and they, if they get a route which is not the right route the client likes, so it's basically I am the man who has to be blamed for everything. So, canceled flight, they didn't get their food in on the plane, so **it's my fault**. If the plane didn't take off on time, it's my fault. If there was a snow and their car couldn't reach the airport so it's my fault. Uh, it's-it's pretty interesting that how, uh, being an agent, you take the responsibility of the client's problems and the airlines' problems. Probably that's what a travel agent is all about. But, it's-it's interesting. I mean, when something happens and you get a call from a client from India in the middle of the night saying, "The airline is not allowing me to fly," you can't do, you can't fly to India to bring him but you **deal with it**. Yeah, I mean, if-if one is not a people person, you can easily have a high-high blood pressure, most of the time, you die with a heart attack, but I think it's-it's interesting to me.

It's very hard to, uh, uh, **fire** people—uh, hiring is always a very-very pleasant feeling, that you—as if you are giving employment to people and people come with a lot of requests and they-they-they feel happy if you say, "C'mon." But I-I, initially I had a lot of problem in, uh, because I am, I always trusted people, whatever information they gave on, but then eventually you find out that the person is not the kind of person you want and you're not giving them a best job in the world, so, uh, they're also not with you forever so there's a very high **turnover** so I have, I had a hard time firing few people. I never told anybody that "I fire you," but eventually they also realize that they don't have a future here so they go move away. I never had to fire someone, I never had to say, "Get out, you don't have a job here." But I guess they-they also read from my face and I'm-I-I'm-I-I tell them that "You're not performing well, improve yourself."

But now, in, uh, **Subway**, I have, uh, decided that I-I take a lot of time in hiring, so that I eventually don't have to make them feel they are not good for the job so I have to raise their salary, I have to give them incentives, I have to give lot of training. It's-it's a very difficult, uh, people, uh, employing and-and keeping them on, it's very difficult.

4. THE CPA

CPA: My customers that I deal with are fellow employees, personnel, and helping them with issues. I don't directly have contact with our clients that our customer service people have contact with, unless there's a really big problem, uh, which normally has to do with collections but, um. . . . But generally I consider my customers are the fellow employees as, 'cause I'm also in charge of some personnel and helping, and make sure that they're happy because if your employees are happy, they will then make your customers happy so that's truly my customers.

I mean, I'm recently started helping an employee who I noticed was having some personal issues and she and I, you know, talked one day, and I was thinking, you know, "She needs to talk to somebody professionally." And so I reminded her of an employee benefit that we had where you can get free counseling. So I, you know, gave her the phone number and all I could do was just encourage her to call, couldn't make her call, couldn't require her to call. But I, um, just tried to, you know, convince her to call, and she did and she called and so now she and I check up on each other like once a week or sometimes once a day. At first it was like once a day and she would tell me that she called and how everything was going and that made me proud, you know, as-as a manager, as a friend, you know, as another fellow coworker and just as a human being, to know that, you know, this person was screaming for help and no one heard 'em. And the fact that I was **in tune** enough to pick up on that and, you know, get her the help that she needed and she's still, you know, going and we-we check up every few days, once a week and so. . . .

IT PROFESSIONAL: She can do her job again.

CPA: Yeah, now she can function with her, you know, with her job and, um, she's doing—and she's still getting— every week, she's making more and more, you know, progress and **working out.**

5. THE HOTEL MANAGER

Absolutely, there is technique for this, if you have any problem with any client in a hotel for any reason, you have to know how to talk to them. So, first step, you have to listen. You have to learn to listen and this is very, very important step. So you have to listen what the problem is, very carefully. After you hear all the problem, you can ask some question to clear-**clarify** the problems with the client. After you got all information from the client, you thank them and you have to **follow up,** you not stop for a minute. Follow up what happened in this problem and you have to get it done, and after you get it done, you go back to the client and make sure he's satisfied, make sure he's very happy before he leaves the hotel. So it's very, very special technique and I took seminars in this technique and I'm working in it, because, as background, it's very hard to listen, you know, it's very hard. It's very easy to talk. But listening is-is-is-is the technique you have to learn and, uh, sometimes I forget myself and so you interrupt the client but I go back again to my technique. You have to just keep listening because listening is number one technique to solve this problems.

6. THE MECHANIC

INTERVIEWER: Who are your clientele on a given day?

MECHANIC: Customers?

INTERVIEWER: Uh-huh.

MECHANIC: Uh, it's-it's a variety of races: um, black, white, Chinese, Spanish, um. Some people are just hard to deal with, some people are nice to deal with. Some people give you tips, some people just, are just **snotty** about it.

INTERVIEWER: So how do you deal with people who, how do you deal with a problem customer, how do you handle that?

MECHANIC: Um, you try to keep a calm voice, try to calm them down and make sure whatever they want, they get. And just make sure they're happy so they keep coming back and giving you business.

INTERVIEWER: Do you have many problem customers or have you had many problem customers since you've been working here?

MECHANIC: Uh, I've had **a handful** of them. I'm not really the one that takes care of the customers, I'm out in the garage 'cause I'm a shop foreman and I take care of all of the, um, the general service people that are below me. And if a customer comes out and asks questions, I step in and take over and make sure the customer feels satisfied that we're taking care of their-their car right.

INTERVIEWER: Can you think of one example, one recent occurrence?

MECHANIC: Um, a recent occurrence that just happened like yesterday was, I was washing the floors and I was **kinda** dirty so when I got into a person's car to take it out of the-the garage, I got a little grease on the door and I didn't wipe it up—I didn't see it—and the customer complained about it, and I just went ahead and took care of it and cleaned it up for **'em**.

7. THE **EMT**

Um, initially I just make sure I don't make a problem of myself and first, not to **escalate a situation**, try to find a means to, um, come to some type of understanding with the people that you're dealing with and-and **maintain positivity**, no matter how negative someone else may get, no matter how, you know, bad a person may conduct themselves, don't allow that to taint you and you become negative. You stay positive, you keep your focus and stay calm. Don't be confrontational, stay calm, and, um, just try to, try to understand, you know or help somebody to understand what's going on **wit chu**.

8. THE **IT** PROFESSIONAL

IT PROFESSIONAL: I have basically a pro—, there's a project management, which is in-house, and there's, uh, um, and my IT **lead**, who is a senior—more a senior—developer than I am.

INTERVIEWER: Uh-huh.

IT PROFESSIONAL: Uh, I deal directly with him, he usually will shield me from requests coming from project management, which, in turn, have come from the client.

INTERVIEWER: Uh-huh.

IT PROFESSIONAL: That has been an ongoing battle through all of **corporate America** for probably bill—, eons, eons, and eons, since it's ever . . .

INTERVIEWER: What do you mean?

IT PROFESSIONAL: Uh, y—, we, there's a chain of command in the business world and as chores are passed down to workers, uh, inevitably things get **mixed up**, OK? And if something gets mixed up, then either blame could be placed or, uh, problem, uh, different problems arise and things happen, so, uh, the, in our particular instance, the scenario is, well, what was the requirement? And if-if my answer as the worker, the IT professional says, "Well, we never were, we were never given requirements, they just said, 'Make it **sorta** look like this.'" But we needed a document that said, "Hey, I wanted this information programmed in a certain **font**," for instance. And they didn't give us that font and we don't know that font, then it's gonna show up the way we want it to show up, not the way the client may want it to **show up**.

INTERVIEWER: Right.

IT PROFESSIONAL: The issue—the problems that arise from that—is that project management, who deals with the clients, uh, doesn't, may not get us the information, and if they don't get us the information then, this back and forth and there's bickering and you know, people are placing blame and we were trying to figure out—I think this has probably been going on for thousands of years—

people want to figure out how to work this so that that doesn't happen.

And, you know, you go, you go about your business in the most pleasant manner that you can and you do your job and you prepare for these things so that you can **cover yourself**. And everybody knows that you're gonna eventually have to do that. At some point in time, you're definitely gonna have to do that.

9. THE ENTREPRENEUR

ENTREPRENEUR: Always—and I think it's the more people that you deal with, you know. If you can keep 99 percent of the people happy, that means one in a hundred you're gonna have a hard time with, so, if you only deal with a hundred people in the course of a week, well then you only have **one rotten apple**. Now, if you deal with a thousand people in the course of a week. My brother at the tattoo shop has been there for ten years. Now, ten years ago, we did ten thousand people, so in the course of a year, maybe there was ten disgruntled customers.

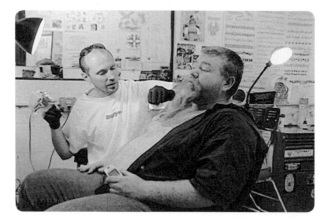

Now we have ten disgruntled customers every month. Well, we're dealing with, you know, a hundred thousand people.

INTERVIEWER: What, it's-it's changed, simply because of the increa⎡sed numbers⎤?

ENTREPRENEUR: ⎣   Sure.   ⎦

INTERVIEWER: Or is it because people are more aware ⎡of their rights and . . .⎤

ENTREPRENEUR: ⎣Increase in numbers—⎦the percentage is still the same. You know, if you can maintain a 99 percent happiness average, I think you're doing pretty good. I used to **beat myself to death** and try to keep everybody happy and then this wise man, Bob Simpson, once told me this story about the man and the son and the donkey going to market. Do you know the story?

INTERVIEWER: Uh, go ahead.

ENTREPRENEUR: There's a-a farmer's taking his donkey to sell him at market and he takes his son along so the three of them are walking down the street. They pass the first little village and some people—they overhear some people—saying, "Look at that grown man pulling that donkey and making his son walk. Why doesn't he have the son ride the donkey?" So he puts his son up on the donkey. Well, they come to the next group of people and they overhear 'em saying, "Look at that disrespectful boy: he's riding that donkey when his father should be up there." So they switch positions, they get to the next town, and they hear some people saying, you know, "Look at that man burdening that poor donkey when he's perfectly capable of walking."

INTERVIEWER: You've had to hire and fire people?

ENTREPRENEUR: I don't think I've ever really said to someone, "You're fired," but it got to the point where they weren't performing at their job so then I put the pressure on them to **shape up or ship out**, as the phrase goes and, uh, I guess you could say in essence I fired 'em but not directly; indirectly through putting pressure on them to get the job done and if they weren't performing, then they were unhappy to the point where they eventually quit.

DEFINITIONS

beat myself to death: To berate or blame oneself excessively.

bend to the will: To do what another person wants, usually achieved by pressure or coercion.

CAT scan (or CT scan; Computerized Axial Tomography): A diagnostic x-ray procedure that combines, with the aid of a computer, many x-ray images taken from different angles to generate cross-sectional or three-dimensional views of specific parts of the human body.

'cause: Common shortened pronunciation of *because*.

clearify: In standard English, *clarify*.

corporate America: A reference to the American business world or culture.

cover yourself: To protect yourself, to be able to justify your actions.

crooked: In this context, dishonest or unethical, even criminal.

deal with it: To take care of the problem or situation at hand.

'em: Common shortened pronunciation of *them*.

emergency room: The department of a hospital that provides urgent care to seriously ill or injured persons, now more frequently referred to as the emergency department in many places.

EMT (Emergency Medical Technician): An allied health professional who is responsible for responding to medical emergencies and providing initial first-aid care and transportation of the sick or injured persons to a medical facility.

escalate a situation: To make a situation more intense or worse.

fall short: To fail to meet expectations or to have a result or outcome that did not meet the desired goal or requirements.

fire: To terminate a person from employment.

follow up: To check on a situation after an initial action was taken to determine if the desired result was achieved.

font: A style of typeface.

fork in the road: A point at which a choice or decision has to be made between two alternatives.

gonna: Going to.

a handful: A common expression meaning a small number, or "a few."

I'da: Common contraction and pronunciation of *I would have*.

in tune: In this context, to be aware of something or someone's needs.

IT (Information Technology): Equipment, devices, or infrastructure used for transmitting, storing, or processing electronic data.

it's my fault: I'm responsible for what happened or went wrong.

kinda: Kind of.

lead: The person directing the project

maintain positivity: To keep a positive outlook or attitude.

mixed up: Confused, in a state of disarray, out of order.

nub: This speaker's description of a bump or swelling.

on the up and up: Legitimate or trustworthy.

one rotten apple: A person who is the only unhappy or dissatisfied person among a group of people, or a troublemaker.

one-stone kill: Solving a problem with one single effort, technique, or approach. (Not a common American expression.)

painkillers: Medication designed to reduce pain.

primary care physicians: Doctors who are responsible for overseeing the general health care needs of people.

shape up or ship out: To do what is correct or expected or leave.

show up: In this context, to appear.

snotty: Slang for *indignant, nasty, unpleasant.*

sorta: Sort of.

Subway: A fast-food chain that specializes in submarine sandwiches.

team approach: A group of individuals working to achieve the same goal or objective.

told 'em: Common pronunciation of *told them*.

turnover: Change in the employees who work at a business due to employees being hired and fired, or leaving by their own choice.

unheard of: Unusual or uncommon.

wholistic care: All-inclusive health care (not standard and not to be confused with *holistic*).

wit chu: A colloquial pronunciation of *with you*.

work ethic: A person's disposition, attitude, or approach to his or her work.

working out: In this context, succeeding, or having the desired result or outcome.

QUESTIONS AND EXERCISES

1. List some of the problems encountered by the speakers.

2. Describe how speakers handle problems.

3. With whom have speakers had problems?

4. Describe your problems at work. Were they with coworkers? With customers?

5. Describe the problems that a friend, coworker, or classmate has had at work.

6. How do you solve problems at work?

7. Identify three words or phrases in this chapter that are new to you, and write a sentence with each one.

CHAPTER 10

TECHNOLOGY AT WORK

In this chapter, interviewees describe the various kinds of technology they use to do their jobs.

1. THE UNIVERSITY PROFESSOR (LINGUISTICS)

Lots of video, lots of digital video, um, I'd say that's probably the-the biggest one. And b—, since this is Gallaudet, a deaf university, we use a lot of technology that is **deaf-friendly** or that makes, uh, the visual component of the classroom more accessible for students, say, who want to come back and review the course—the class—that we just had, uh, say, today. They, those are filmed—those are videotaped automatically—and then uploaded to our course website and the students can go and watch those, review things that I had said. They can look at what's on the board. The **PowerPoint** slides that I had are also integrated so we have a lot of that, I guess, assistive or enhancing technology here at Gallaudet.

2. THE CHEMIST

The computer, uh, a BlackBerry, cell phone—the Black-Berry which is kind of like, in a way, a bane to humankind because it's-it's very useful, but then people always think that you are always looking at your **e-mail**, you know, so "I can send something at ten o'clock and maybe she'll look at it," at night, you know, and sometimes, unfortunately, I am, you know, they can send me . . . I'm terrible, "What am I doing?!" So, but it, in a way it's also helpful because on the subway in the morning, um, I can take a quick look and see what's-what's coming up because, you know, there are people who start at seven in the morning. I'm not one of them, I'm, you know, an eight-thirty in the morning person, so, and my boss is a seven in the morning person, so, you know, I also get a number of e-mails from him while he's **fresh and bushy-tailed**.

3. THE ACCOUNTANT

INTERVIEWER: Do you like being able to be connected all the time, anywhere?

ACCOUNTANT: No. It's very conve—, I just got a phone that does e-mail. It's very convenient to be able to check that. You know, for example, today I was on the bus going to work and I could check my e-mail before work. That was convenient. Uh, I do not want to be **connected** all the time, uh, but it is awfully convenient and I-I'm gonna have to watch that. Uh, but they're paying for it. You know, the company pays for me to have e-mail on my phone, so I can't just turn it off. Uh, but it mostly gets turned off on weekends, it does not go upstairs, it stays downstairs, uh, yeah. But it's-it's very convenient and it's-it's—I don't tend to respond to things, uh, you know, because you have to do **the thing with the thumbs** and I'm not great at that—uh, but it's **awfully nice** to be able to just read the e-mail and know what's coming when I get to work.

Uh, I will never do that while I'm driving, which some people do, uh, but yeah-yeah. Uh, this—the phone that I just got—is also, uh, theo—, hope—, supposed to work worldwide, uh, so in theory, when we go to Venice, it'll work over there, uh, and I'm actually kind of concerned about that. That's good and bad. I want to be able to get that call that says, "The house is **burning down**." I do not want all the normal calls that I would normally get while I'm in Venice. So, some-some filter would be nice.

4. THE ENTREPRENEUR AND THE SURGICAL TECHNOLOGIST

ENTREPRENEUR: Aircraft, computers, people, telephone, mechanical things, automatic activation devices on parachutes, the latest parachute technology, uh. That's all I can think of off the top of my head.

SURGICAL TECHNOLOGIST: We use a lot of computers. Um, all of the charting and things, like, are starting to go, instead of on paper, they're on computer now. Uh, video monitors, we have flat-screen TVs now, uh, for our laparoscopic procedures. Um, yeah, telephones. I'm sure it'll-it'll just keep increasing from there. You know, there's robots that are starting to do surgery and—we don't have that yet but—I'm-I'm sure that's where we're headed.

5. THE **EMT**

EMT: Various things, like I mentioned, uh, earlier: **EKG** machine, which we use to check the, um, electrical activity of a person's heart to see that everything is flowing correctly, um, we use monitors, which we connect to a person so that we can constantly observe their heart flow, heart activity, uh, everything from the basic stretchers that we push and **break our backs** on every day, uh. It's just a wide—, oxygen tanks, which, you know, it's good to be familiar—usually at the hospital, they're al—, they're already together but, hey, you never know when a situation may occur and it's not together, so you need to know. Uh, basic thermometers, scales, it's a wide range of equipment that-that we use, it's a wide range of things.

INTERVIEWER: And I imagine that in some way you have-have to use computers?

EMT: Absolutely. **Computers is**-is a very important part of the hospital because of tracking, a means to-to keep track of patients, uh, means of putting in information and retrieving information. It's extremely vital so that's something else that is good, if a person might be able t— jus— type a little bit, **y'know**, ten words a minute, y'know, you don't have to be a secretary or extraordinary on the keys, but if you-you can read, type a little bit, you're good, 'cause in most cases, most of what I see on the most basic level, if a person can read at least on a tenth-grade level, they can get a grasp of this information.

6. THE TRAVEL AGENT

I mean, technology is-is big time because when I have **Subway** now, I-I move, I take, carry my—it's not a cell phone, it's like a, um, phone over Internet, uh, I think **VOIP**, something—and, uh, I carry that phone wherever I go. If I'm home, the phone rings at home; if I'm in my Subway, it rings there; if I'm here, it works here. So technology, of c—, it's a big—I mean, uh, if I was in any other country, even in India, I don't think, they don't have a technology like we have here in U.S. And uh, I have nothing else—my-my-my inventory is computer. I mean, all the tickets, central reservation system, I can do only reservations. If I don't have a computer, it's practically impossible. So high-speed Internet and connections, it's networking, technology. I mean, my travel agency work on technology. If I have no technology, I mean, I-I can't go to airline offices and **fetch** the tickets.

7. THE SIGN LANGUAGE INTERPRETER

Technology as far as work goes, uh, let's see. Well, you—as an interpreter—you become experienced, you become comfortable with different types of technology depending on what setting or environment you're going in. Personally, I love technology and so I'm very excited about working with computers, uh, I've recently made the switch from being a **PC** user my entire life to about a year and a half ago going to a Mac environment, an Apple environment, and so, I do a lot of video editing occasionally, when I have free time, which involves taking movies that I've made, uh, personal movies from home—taking them and converting them to **DVD**s, um, pretty much becoming a producer, if you will, for fun. And so I'm familiar with a lot of video editing technology, uh, of course, **PDA**s, personal data assistants, I use a lot as an interpreter. For years as an interpreter I traveled, uh, using a book, having a-a calendar but as technology's progressed, it's become a lot easier to use a **Palm Pilot** or a PDA, um, for your e-mail, for your scheduling, and so forth. Uh, other technology I would use, uh, I would say it's just cell phone, cameras, that type of thing and just being familiar with the different technology that's out there so that if you're in an interpreting situation and you—terms are being used—you need to be familiar with current technology so that you can make the appropriate interpretation into, uh, sign language or English.

DEFINITIONS

awfully nice: A common colloquial expression that means "very nice."

break our backs: To do difficult physical labor.

burning down: Being consumed by fire.

computers is: In standard grammatical English, this would be *computers are.*

connected: Here used in the sense of being accessible by various digital communication technologies.

deaf-friendly: Something that accommodates deaf people or is easy for deaf people to use.

DVD: digital versatile disk.

EKG (also **ECG; Electrocardiogram**)**:** A diagnostic test used to evaluate the performance of the heart by monitoring its electrical activity and producing a graphic trace of that electrical activity on paper.

e-mail (electronic mail): Printed matter that is transmitted electronically.

EMT (Emergency Medical Technician): An allied health professional who is responsible for responding to medical emergencies and providing initial first-aid care and transportation of the sick or injured persons to a medical facility.

fetch: Means "to get." Most Americans say "get." This term is more commonly used in the southern United States. However, it is not limited to non-American English or southern American speech.

fresh and bushy-tailed (or **bright-eyed and bushy-tailed**)**:** Alert and ready.

Palm Pilot: A specific brand of PDA.

PC: Personal computer.

PDA: personal digital assistant.

PowerPoint: Brand of digital slide presentation.

Subway: A fast-food chain that specializes in submarine sandwiches.

the thing with the thumbs: This is a reference to the way people usually use their thumbs when entering information or sending messages from a PDA or BlackBerry.

VOIP (Voice Over Internet Protocol): Technology that allows a person's voice to be transmitted over the Internet.

y'know: Colloquial pronunciation of *you know.*

QUESTIONS AND EXERCISES

1. Which job described in this chapter requires the most technology?

2. List the kinds of technology used by these speakers.

3. How do these speakers feel about the use of technology for their jobs?

4. What kind of technology do you use for your job and how do you feel about it?

5. What kind of technology does a friend, coworker, or classmate use for his or her job?

6. What do you see as the future of technology at work?

7. Identify three words or phrases in this chapter that are new to you, and write a sentence with each one.